# God Found

LIAM GOLIGHER

BARBARA LADDS

GHILLEAN PRANCE

MORWEN HIGHAM

JOEL EDWARDS

CHRISTOPHER  IDLE

MARIE-CHRISTINE LUX

OLIVER McALLISTER

LINDSAY BENN

TIM TRUMPER

PRITTI GURNEY

BOB AKROYD

For
Diane, Craig and Scott

# God Found Me

### Edited by Irene Howat

## Christian Focus

ISBN 1 85792 238 7

© Christian Focus Publications

Published in 2000
by
Christian Focus Publications
Geanies House, Fearn,
Ross-shire, IV20 1TW, Great Britain

Cover design by Owen Daily

Printed and bound in Great Britain by
Cox & Wyman Ltd, Reading, Berkshire

# Contents

# ACKNOWLEDGEMENTS

I would like to thank the contributors to this book. It has been a privilege working with them. My thanks is also due to those who have upheld the project in prayer. Please continue to do so, praying that these testimonies may be used by God to bring others to faith, that they too might bear testimony to the saving grace of the Lord Jesus Christ.

Irene Howat

# THEY MET JESUS

Have you met Jesus? The fishermen Andrew and Peter met him on the shore of the Lake Galilee. They dropped what they were doing and followed him. When Zacchaeus, a taxman and crook, met Jesus, he gave back fourfold the money he had swindled. They and many others met Jesus, the wandering preacher from Nazareth, during his three years of public ministry. But that is not surprising. After all, as Jesus never strayed all that far from home, they were likely to bump into him at some point of his travels. That they met him was nothing unusual, but what is surprising is that the record of the impact Jesus had on them is still in print and read today, two millennia later.

Thomas met Jesus too, and in quite extraordinary circumstances because it was after Jesus had been killed by public crucifixion. Dozens – perhaps hundreds – of people had gathered to watch the spectacle. Soldiers, experienced in carrying out executions, checked his body for life, and there was none. There was no mistake. Jesus was dead. A week later Thomas heard that Jesus had appeared to his friends! Doubter that he was, he announced that he wouldn't believe it until he could touch the crucifixion wounds on Jesus' hands and side. Then Thomas met the risen Jesus for himself. Did he reach out his hands to touch the wounds? No. Thomas, who had known Jesus for some years, had no need to do that. His eyes and his heart recognised the living Lord. 'My Lord and my God!' he breathed in wonder.

Jesus is no longer constrained to an earthly body, or to a wandering ministry in Palestine. Over the last two thousand years men, women and young people throughout the world have met Jesus. Some have turned their backs on him and walked away, consigning him to history or myth. But those who have believed, even those like Thomas for whom believing was a problem, have found him to be their Lord and their God. The contributors to this book are among that vast number of people who have met Jesus, and who have found him to be their redeemer and friend.

When Jesus meets people, he deals with them as individuals. That should not surprise us, after all he made us as individuals. Consequently each account in the book is very different from the others.

**LIAM GOLIGHER** and his wife, Christine, have five children. Prior to his present pastorate in Kirkintilloch in Scotland, Liam ministered in Northern Ireland and in Canada. He is a popular conference speaker. Those who attend the

Keswick Convention know Liam well and appreciate his expository style of preaching. His book, *A Window on Tomorrow*, shows something of Liam's wonder at the prospect of the Lord's second coming. That wonder is evident in his preaching, which is both winsome and urgent.

**BARBARA LADDS** lives in Belfast. She and her husband, Mark, have four children. After a Christian upbringing, Barbara rebelled in her teens. She moved to Peterborough where she married young. Her marriage to Mark went through troubled times, and was reaching breaking point when he became a believer. Her family and home church were prayerful for her, and their prayers were answered when she came to faith. At last she and Mark had something in common, a saving faith in Jesus.

**GHILLEAN PRANCE**, who was brought up in the country, first in Skye then in Gloucestershire, was interested in botany from childhood. Very soon after he went to Oxford to study the subject of his passion, he became a Christian. The following summer he met Anne, whom he later married. They have two daughters. After working in America and Brazil, where he became deeply involved in ecological issues, Ghillean returned to England to become Director of the Royal Botanic Gardens, Kew.

**MORWEN HIGHAM** is married to Vernon, who is pastor of Heath Evangelical Church, Cardiff. They have three children. Morwen is Welsh through and through. Her testimony takes readers from the influence of her godly grandparents, who were the fruit of a Welsh Revival, through her conversion when a young woman, her training and work as a Sister of the People, to her present situation, as wife and helpmeet to Vernon. They have served the Lord together for over forty years.

**JOEL EDWARDS** studied at London Bible College, then worked as a Probation Officer. He served as the first General Secretary of the African and Caribbean Evangelical Alliance, and as UK Director of the Evangelical Alliance before his appointment as EA's General Director in 1997. He is also an ordained minister of the New Testament Church of God. Joel is married to Carol and they have two children Joel Jnr and Davina.

**CHRISTOPHER IDLE** lives in south east London, having retired there after thirty years in full-time ministry in the Church of England. He and his wife Marjory belong to Christ Church, Old Kent Road. They are both authors, and both involved in local schools. Much of Christopher's work is connected with hymns, of which he has written some three hundred. Their four sons, three of them married, are based in England, but have worked in a variety of far flung places.

**MARIE CHRISTINE LUX**'s story spans the world. Born in the then Belgian Congo, she moved to Belgium as a teenager. From there she set off on further travels, first in the Merchant Navy then to Australia and Tasmania, where she was converted. After training as a nurse, Marie-Christine often had her passport stamped as she travelled in the Lord's service. She has worked in Somalia, India, Peru and the Central African Republic. Marie-Christine is now serving with Tear Fund in Honduras.

**OLIVER McALLISTER** and his wife, Deirdre, live in Randalstown, Northern Ireland. They have three daughters. The death of his father had a profound effect on Oliver, who was then eleven years old. He found no comfort in the Roman Catholic faith of his childhood. Although he was challenged by the gospel as a young man, it was years later that God broke through the barriers Oliver had built up, and called him to saving faith and a life of service.

**LINDSAY BENN** lives in Eastbourne, where her husband, Wallace, serves as Bishop of Lewes. The Benns have two children. Having been brought up in a Christian home, Lindsay came to a personal faith in Jesus as a schoolgirl. After she qualified as a teacher, Wallace and Lindsay married. Her training in working with young people was put to use in the youth work they did together. The Benns have found God faithful in their various congregations and through difficult family situations.

**TIM TRUMPER** is a Welshman, the son of a preacher. Although he always believed that what the Bible taught was true, it was when he was fifteen years old and at a Christian youth camp, that Tim accepted God's offer of forgiveness and new life. As a boy, Tim was determined not to be a preacher. The Lord thought differently. After university, Tim studied theology and he is now Assistant Professor of Systematic Theology at Westminster Theological Seminary in Philadelphia.

**PRITTI GURNEY** was born into a Hindu family and spent the first nineteen years of her life in Leicester. In 1989 she went to Leeds Metropolitan University to train as a teacher. After graduating, she worked in a primary school in Leeds for three and a half years, during which time she married Marcus. At present she is enjoying being a housewife. Marcus and Pritti live near Wetherby in North Yorkshire. They worship at King's Church in Boston Spa.

**BOB AKROYD,** who is married to Heather, is an American from New Jersey. After graduating from university, he went to Tokyo where he taught English to Japanese businessmen. In 1990 Bob moved to Edinburgh to study for his PhD. It was there that he first met the challenge of the gospel and after much heart searching came to faith. Studies in theology followed, and Bob is now an assistant minister in the Free Church of Scotland.

The contributors to this book have all met with the living and loving Lord. Have you met Jesus?

# LIAM GOLIGHER

Though it may sound like arrogance to say it, it is the simple truth: I cannot remember a time when I did not love the Lord Jesus. I use the word 'love' quite deliberately, for my love of Jesus preceded my understanding, my act of faith and my growing obedience to him. For as long as I can remember he has been a part of my life. From my earliest days he was a presence spoken of naturally and without affect by those around me. Then, as I grew up, I found him to be an ever present friend. Now, with the passing of time and the maturing of faith, he is an even closer presence and an even better friend, one whom I approach with awe and wonder, knowing him to be my Lord and God.

The earliest Christian influences I can remember came from my mother's family. Her brother was a minister in the United Free Church of Scotland, her sister a missionary in Argentina. And my grandmother, a real Mother in Israel, always had her home full of people involved in Christian service. I spent many happy hours listening to the conversations that went on around me, enthralled at the stories they had to tell about the Lord's work.

## A happy home in Hamilton

When I was four years old we moved to Hamilton where life could be quite tough at times. We were housed on the top floor of a condemned tenement block – and when the ceiling fell in, we moved to the middle flat. That was a step up in the world as it was a bigger flat! We had an outside toilet, and I have vivid memories of breaking the ice on the water and staring up at the stars on a frosty night. In spite of our privations, my family was happy. Mother taught us to be content, remembering that we were rich in the things that money could not buy.

During these years we were accepted into the family at Hamilton Baptist Church and made to feel most welcome. The Junior Christian Endeavour Society was of paramount importance to me, influencing the early stages of my Christian awakening and growth. It was there I learned the importance of reading the Bible, praying and memorising Scripture verses. And it was through CE that I had my first experiences of 'going public' in church services. Giving short talks, reading Scripture, praying and leading meetings were all precursors to what was to be my life's work.

Another important development in my early

life was my emergent love of reading. This was due to my father's habit of buying me the *Classics Illustrated*. These were the great classical works of Dickens, Dumas, Bronte and others printed in comic form for children. Such was their effect that I took myself to the library to get the original works to read. I read five novels a week, the maximum number allowed on my parents' tickets from the 'grown up library'!

## Dr. Billy Graham ... and mimic
When I was about twelve years old, my father took me to the Maranatha Centre in Motherwell to see a Billy Graham film. The sight of Dr. Graham explaining the gospel so clearly and forcefully gripped my imagination. I went home and repeated the sermon: actions, accent, everything, to a congregation of one ... my younger brother perched on the upper bunk bed! He still remembers my early experimentation in the art of preaching! From then on my visits to the library took a new direction. I decided to read every book in the theological section. Some were a bit beyond me – I remember struggling a bit with Karl Barth's *Evangelical Theology*! Every penny of my pocket money was spent on theological books. The cows in the fields beyond our home formed the only congregation that would listen to the sermons that I prepared and preached.

I began my story by saying that I cannot remember a time in my life when Jesus was not real to me and that I did not love him. But, while that is true, its reality did not go unchallenged by the evangelicalism of the time. The evangelistic preaching I heard insisted on a date and time of conversion, an identifiable life-changing experience. We sang songs which said 'Years I spent in vanity and pride...' which, in my tender years, did not really reflect my experience! I so longed to have a testimony, to be able to point to a day and an hour when I had received Christ as my Saviour. On a number of occasions I prayed for Jesus to come into my heart. On one such I put my hand up in response to an appeal, and for some time identified that as my conversion. So important did it seem to have a date. While I was sincere in my prayers, I was disappointed in the lack of spiritual fireworks. But, throughout it all, God was developing in me the relationship I already had with the Lord Jesus.

**God gave my young heart courage**
At secondary school my spiritual life was challenged because my contemporaries were violently opposed to the Christian faith. Church was an irrelevance, Christ an expletive. By nature I was rather timid and driven by a desire to please. I wanted to be liked. But a verse of Scripture which spoke to me particularly at that period was,

'If you confess with your mouth, "Jesus is Lord," and believe in your heart that God raised him from the dead, you will be saved' (Romans 10:9). God gave my young heart courage, and from my very early teens I was enabled to speak out in school debates and classroom discussions. I soon became known as a Christian. While that was a privilege, it brought trouble from the boys in my class. Giving me a kicking became something of a pastime for them. In spite of that, I had many opportunities at school to speak about the Christian faith. Looking back I can see why I was a target for the bullies!

Before I was fifteen, I had discovered a whole new theological world. As I read Scripture, I found myself asking serious questions about its key themes. Then, in the Free Presbyterian Bookshop in Glasgow, I found some books which put into words the very conclusions I was reaching. They introduced me to names like McCheyne, Bonar, Spurgeon and Whitefield. The doctrines of grace fed my mind and warmed my heart, giving further impetus to the evangelistic zeal first sparked by Billy Graham. I debated my new found discoveries with my friends at church who must have thought at times I was a bit 'off the wall'. For some time I thought that I was the only person who believed these great doctrines of grace. Then I was taken to the Tent Hall in Glasgow, where I listened enthralled as Dr.

Martyn Lloyd Jones preached on things that 'cannot be shaken' (Hebrews 12:27). At last I had found a present day preacher of the theology I had come to espouse.

## Taking Spurgeon's advice

On leaving school in 1966, aged fifteen, I applied to the SMT bus company for a job as an assistant to the auditor. At my interview I explained to the Chief Executive that, if given the job, I would only be there for a few years as I wanted to be an evangelist. He laughed, thanked me for my honesty, and said I had just the qualities needed to be an Assistant Auditor, this despite maths having been my worst subject at school! Part of my reason for entering the world of work was that C H Spurgeon had emphasised that men going into the ministry needed to have a thorough experience of the secular environment. I enjoyed my job and continued my education at night school before going to Langside College in 1968 where I studied for my Highers. While there I had the inestimable privilege of Christian friends from many different denominations. Together we started a Christian Union, and attended the Strathpeffer Convention. I came to appreciate the distinctive emphases of Christians from different denominations and, to this day, I feel most comfortable in an interdenominational setting.

In 1968 I applied to the Baptist Union of

Scotland to be considered as a candidate for the ministry. But, having applied, I started having doubts about my suitability. It was the support of my friends that helped me to clarify my understanding of God's will for my life. Reading one morning of Jeremiah's reaction to God's call, '"Ah, Sovereign Lord," I said, "I do not know how to speak; I am only a child," and God's answer to him, "Get yourself ready! Stand up and say to them whatever I command you"' (Jeremiah 1:6, 17), I felt it reflected my own situation. Like Jeremiah, I felt too young to be entrusted with preaching God's Word. But, that very same day when a friend invited me home for lunch, his wife told me she had been praying for me that morning and felt that God was directing me to Jeremiah Chapter 1. That evening, in St. Vincent Free Church, the preacher spoke from Jeremiah chapter 1! I got the message loud and clear, and I have never since doubted God's call to me to preach his Word. 'The Lord said to me, "Do not say 'I am only a child'." You must go to everyone I send you to and say whatever I command you' (Jeremiah 1:7). How important I found it to be to have my call to preach confirmed by the words of Scripture. It is a reliable anchor when tossed about on the sea of adversity and doubt, criticism and discouragement, failure and sin.

**The work of an evangelist**

I became involved in various forms of Christian evangelistic outreach. And I think it would be true to say that my greatest burden then, as it is now, was to 'do the work of an evangelist' (2 Timothy 4:5). Some friends who had formed a Christian music band invited me to join them on their tours as their 'resident speaker'. Our bookings were varied, from visiting coffee bars to being the 'entertainment' at dances. What splendid opportunities this afforded to tell the good news of the gospel in a non Christian setting. We saw a number of people come to know the Lord through a local coffee bar in Hamilton in which we worked. About that time (1969/70) the Jesus Movement reached Britain, with its modern songs, contemporary clothes and its ability to reach a rebellious generation. It seemed to me to be the perfect expression of vital Christianity. I hope I never lose that vision of a Christian faith that is geared to the skies while anchored to the rock, committed to the unchanging Word of God, yet able to respond flexibly to the changing cultural trends of our times.

In September 1970, I set out for Belfast and theological training at the Irish Baptist College. There I received a thorough foundation in Systematic Theology and Church History, and was given a rigorous framework for Biblical exegesis. I'm afraid I nearly drove the Hebrew and Greek lecturers to despair! And it was while I was in Belfast that I met a young lady, Christine, who was hoping to go to Africa. Instead she became a minister's wife. Mine. Christine has brought her own blend of devotion and personal integrity to the work of each of the churches in which we have served. She has, from day to day, been a true partner in the work of the gospel. I am grateful for her readiness to prick the bubble of my ego and to challenge me regularly on spiritual issues. I praise God for her personal integrity and spiritual consistency.

## An expository preaching ministry

At the age of twenty-two I started my first pastorate at Rathcoole Baptist Church in Northern Ireland where I was expected to preach four sermons a week. What on earth would I preach about? I asked myself! I soon realised that the best way was to take a book of the Bible and preach through it. This was the beginning of an expository preaching ministry. During my early months in Rathcoole, John Stott, then Rector of All Souls in London, visited Belfast. His coming was formative in confirming for me the need for a regular and systematic exposition of the Bible as an essential foundation to an 'all round' Biblical ministry. While there, some lasting convictions about the church developed in my thinking. Having always loved Jesus, I came to

23

love Jesus' church. The understanding I gained in those days makes me very hesitant to be critical or condemnatory about any aspect of Christ's church. And the shape of a biblical church began to grow in my mind. I came to see a working eldership, a ministering body, contemporary worship, expository preaching and a social conscience as essential ingredients of a fellowship that is spiritually alive.

In many ways I have spent the rest of my ministry trying to put that initial vision into practice. Our time in Ireland was followed by a period in Canada, where we enjoyed rich fellowship with God's people in Cambridge, Ontario. We saw people converted there and the church grew. And it was also there that I was first introduced to working with a church staff. But it has probably been in Kirkintilloch that I have seen my early dreams come to fruition, and fully appreciated what can be done where there is a leadership walking in step with the Spirit and committed to change. God has given us here a group of spiritually-minded leaders whose desire is to obey the Word of God and be open to the wind of the Spirit. This has made possible both church growth and a degree of church renewal. I am grateful for the privilege of working with such an exciting congregation.

**Family matters**

The greatest joy that Christine and I have had in our lives has been our five children. Having a busy home and going through the ups and downs of parenthood has, at times, stretched our faith. One important lesson we learned early on in our role as parents was taught by the great preacher, William Still of Aberdeen. He warned against the danger of Christian parents bringing their children up in fear rather than in faith. That is to say, parents can be overprotective or legalistic because they fear their children will not become believers. But this often has the effect of pushing their children away from them. God has taught us that we should bring our children up in the faith that they will believe. That has made us much more relaxed, especially at those times when they have been exploring the world around them and experimenting with the freedom they have been given. The story is not finished there, of course, but we are grateful to God for the evidences of grace present in the lives of our children.

What about my own personal growth? My experience of the Lord Jesus has been tested, not so much by external events, as by internal and spiritual assaults. Both Satan and my personal propensity to sin have challenged the Lordship of Christ in my life. As the years have passed, God has from time to time shown me the depths of sin to which I could fall, and the heights of grace to which he has lifted me. As a young Christian I could never have conceived of the exceeding sinfulness of sin. But exposure to God's Word has revealed that fundamental corruption which lies in all of us through our connection to Adam. It has taken me years to discover what genuine repentance really involves. An old chorus summarises it well: 'Repentance is to leave the sins we loved before, and show that we in earnest grieve by doing them no more.' I have come to see the depth of corruption latent and active in my own heart, and the length to which God's mercy went in reaching out and saving me. More than I ever did as a young man, I see myself to be a great sinner and in need of a great Saviour.

## What matters

As I have reflected on my Christian journey, a number of convictions have formed in my mind. The first concerns the glory of Christ. The more I study the Bible, the more glorious he becomes. Straddling human history as he does, embodying in himself both the fullness of Godhead and the fullness of man, and being as he is the exalted man of glory, he deserves our most enthusiastic praise and our most thorough obedience. I feel that, in Christian work and service, the greatest motivation to keep going is the knowledge that one day we will 'see the King in his beauty (Isaiah

33:17). On that day, he will be 'glorified in his holy people and ... marvelled at among all those who have believed' (2 Thessalonians 1:10). There are times when, reflecting on that vision, my heart almost feels as if its going to burst with excitement and anticipation. There have been times when I have stood on the hilltop looking out over the horizon and longed for that day when the horizon would disappear and Jesus would reappear. The cover of a book I wrote on the subject, *A Window on Tomorrow*, reflects that thought. It shows a sun setting on the horizon.

The second conviction that I have concerns the sufficiency of the Word of God. Not only has it been a 'lamp to my feet and a light for my path' (Psalm 119:105), but I have seen the Word of God change other people's lives as well, bringing integration and wholeness to some whose lives were coming apart. I have seen it bring people from unorthodoxy to firm Biblical convictions and, above all, I have seen God's Word bring people from spiritual darkness to 'light in the Lord' (Ephesians 5:8). Hesitancy in the pulpit flows, I am sure, from lack of conviction of the sufficiency of holy Scripture.

My third conviction regards the necessity of Christian experience. We sometimes shy away from the word 'experience' because it conjures up images of excess and error. But that is to throw the baby out with the bath water. All Christians

27

have experience of God, or they are not Christians at all. But everyone's experience is different. God deals with us as individuals, and we therefore cannot replicate someone else's experience. There have been times in my life when the Word of God has been underscored or heightened to me by what I can only describe as visions. I have always hesitated to describe these publicly because they are too sacred to me. The experience has sometimes been one of overwhelming conviction, a felt sense of the trueness of some truth, the rightness of some advice or the wrongness of some form of behaviour. In my late teens I sought earnestly to be 'filled with the Spirit'. I don't know what I expected, but what I got was an overwhelming assurance that I was Christ's, a boldness in public speaking and witness that wasn't there before, and a zeal that burned inside me for God and his work. Because experiences can betray us, they must always be checked against the authority of Scripture. But Christian experience must never be denied, for God has made us with minds and feelings as well as wills.

And my last conviction regards the importance of Christian friends. The Puritans used to ask God to give them a spiritual friend who would act as a stimulus to their Christian living, and to be a companion along their Christian way. Over the years I have been blessed with a rich number of friends who have been just that to me. I thank God for the encouragement and guidance they have given me. We were not meant to be solitary in our pilgrimage. One of the dangers in Christian ministry is that we can isolate ourselves in order to maintain a professional aura and to avoid the complications that sometimes arise from relationships. But, if we try to live on our own, we do ourselves an unchristian dis-service.

Recently, when preaching through John's Gospel, I have been thrilled again by the story of Jesus. No-one can compare with him who is his people's Saviour, the world's Lord, the exalted God-man, Jesus Christ.

Jesus, the Name high over all
In hell or earth or sky,
Angels and men before him fall
And devils flee and fly.

Happy if with my latest breath
I may but gasp his Name,
Preach him to all and cry in death
'Behold, behold the Lamb.'

To him alone be glory.

# BARBARA LADDS

Belfast is home to me. I was born there in 1968, one year before the troubles started. I am thankful that no one from our family has been a victim of the violence. God has protected us through all the long years. Ours was a Christian home. My two older brothers and I had the great privilege of having parents, aunts and uncles who were believers. Most of their friends were too.

I loved going to Sunday School and Church. The little choruses we used to sing were very special to me. But, by the age of nine, I had begun to leave these things behind me. Although I was still happy enough to go to church, when I was away from the influence of my parents, I abandoned their standards. And when I was with my friends I didn't care at all about right or wrong, ignoring all my parents had taught me.

## Living life my way
By the time I was fifteen nothing could persuade me to attend Church. I was having a fun time, and church didn't fit into that. Parties and discos did, especially those ones that I wasn't even old

enough to go to. My aim in life was to enjoy myself to the full. And I did. Four years later I was in love. My boyfriend and I agreed to become engaged in the autumn and married the following summer. But before we were engaged we decided on a final fling. He went off on holiday with a friend of his. And I went to Spain with a girl I knew from work.

On the third day of our holiday we met two boys of our own age who came from Peterborough in England. Despite nearly being engaged, I formed a relationship with one of them. I had not gone on holiday with the intention of going out with anyone else, it just happened. Looking back, I can see how God has redeemed even my disloyalty to my boyfriend. But rights and wrongs, and what God wanted, didn't cross my mind at the time. Mark, my friend from Peterborough, and I were inseparable all through our Spanish holiday. We were really upset when the time came for us to part and go home. Would we ever meet again? I asked myself. Or was it just a holiday romance? If it was, I didn't think I'd get over it for a very long time.

Mum knew right away that something was bothering me. Mums just seem to know these things. But even though I told her about Mark I don't think she was prepared for what happened next. I phoned him a few days after arriving back in Belfast. Was it just a holiday romance? No!

He was really pleased to hear me. Before I put the phone down we had started making plans for me to visit Peterborough just two weeks later. My friend from work was to go too. She had fallen for Mark's friend. It seemed that our holiday foursome might turn out to be much more than that. I had a problem to sort out first, a boyfriend to whom I was about to become engaged. It wasn't easy telling him about Mark. But, that hiccup behind me, I planned for the future. I was living life my way.

The visit was a success. Ours was no whirlwind holiday fling. We were in love. Before leaving for Belfast the decision had been made. I would move to Peterborough and live with Mark's parents. 'I'm leaving in two weeks,' I told Mum and Dad. 'And I've handed in my notice at work.' They were devastated. It was an exciting time for me, but things were moving too quickly for them.

### Free at last!
They watched me pack up my things. And I'm sure they prayed their hearts out. Knowing how wilful I had become, they realised that there would be no church connection for me in Peterborough, no Christian influence. I was cutting myself loose from it all. I wanted to be free. In Peterborough I knew I'd be away from the constant restrictions of my Christian

upbringing, and the nagging reminders that Dad and Mum thought I needed to be saved. And I couldn't get away quick enough.

Everything was all right for a while, but I soon realised that I was living in another world. I was able to smoke and drink when and where I wanted. I met all kinds of relationships, different from any I had been used to at home. Divorce was rife. Even very young couples who had been married just a few years were splitting up and heading for divorce. I really wasn't used to this at all. But it was normal for Mark. He had not known even one Christian in his life.

Having wanted to cut free from the standards I'd been brought up with, I couldn't have found a better place to do it. Looking back, it was as though the Lord was showing me that this was the world I'd wanted to live in. Life in Peterborough was very different from life in Belfast. I had a lot to get used to. And I set about making the most of it. We went out every night to the pubs. What a great time we were having!

Just seven months after we met, Mark and I were married in Newtownbreda Baptist Church in Belfast on 27th February 1988. Pastor Sam Simpson, who married us, gave us a Bible. It was to become very special to us in the future, though we wouldn't have believed it at the time. We weren't in the least interested in that sort of thing.

## The bubble bursts

Back in Whittlesey, Peterborough, things were not so good. We were still living with Mark's parents and he went out every night of the week drinking with his mates. I was expecting our first child and I felt very alone. The day our baby was due, Mark went to a party. It was Sunday. I knew what everyone at home would be doing and I felt very homesick indeed. Feeling that no-one cared about me, I told myself over and over again that God cared even if nobody else did. It was to a terribly sad and homesick mum that our first son, Scott, was born. Having a baby brought Mark and me a little closer, but not for long. Fatherhood didn't change him at all. He drank for three solid weeks to celebrate Scott's birth.

We moved into our own house when Scott was six months old. Because it was a bit out of town Mark didn't go drinking in the evenings quite so often. Scott and I were very close. I had nothing else to live for. My life increasingly revolved around my baby as Mark and I grew further and further apart. We had almost nothing in common. And we argued about everything. As the time went on I slid into depression.

Although I had left Mum and Dad, they had not left me. They came to visit us often, even though our constant arguing and bickering nearly drove Mum mad. They knew I was unhappy, but perhaps they did not know how unutterably miserable I really was. In October 1990, as there seemed no prospect of things ever getting any better, I decided to leave Mark and to leave England. Having written a note telling him I would never come back, I got a neighbour to run me to the airport. It was early in the morning, before Mark came home from night shift. But we were late arriving at the airport and missed the plane. 'What can I do?' I pleaded with Mum over the phone. Amid all the hustle and bustle of the airport I felt totally alone. Mum listened. 'Go back home,' she said. 'Go back home.' Knowing that Mark would have read the letter, I had no choice but to go and face the music.

Arriving back at the house about ten o'clock in the morning, I saw him sitting there drowning his sorrows over a twelve-can pack of beer. It was clear he was very upset as he looked twice through the drink to see if it was really us. 'Why did you change your mind?' he asked. 'I didn't,' I replied. 'I missed the plane.' I gave Mark an ultimatum. 'If things don't change by our wedding anniversary, I'm going. And I won't miss the plane.' He had four months to get his act together. In my wildest dreams I couldn't have imagined the changes that would take place by then.

**That's it! I've had enough!**

A month later a night out at a disco ended with a terrible argument between us, and I left the disco. As Mark's parents were minding Scott, it was to their home I went. 'I'm not prepared to wait till February,' I told them. 'I'm going back to Belfast as soon as I can. I'll sort it out in the morning.' In the early hours there was a knock at the door. 'Mark's been knocked down by a car,' a neighbour explained. 'He's lying along there on the road.' His dad and I got into the car and arrived just after the ambulance. 'Barbara, Barbara,' Mark moaned, rolling from side to side on the road. It was obvious that his leg was broken as we could see two raw ends of bone. What we couldn't see was that he also had a fractured skull. It seems terrible to say it, but things had been so bad between us that I wasn't as sympathetic as I should have been. Even as I saw him lying there, I realised it would be up to me to look after Mark when he came out of hospital. And I knew it wouldn't be fun. The life I'd chosen for myself had turned sour.

Mark had surgery to his leg. When he came home a week later, with his leg held together with a plate and screws, he was in terrible pain. If he had been hard to live with before, he was much worse now. But the Lord used this time to speak to Mark. In hospital he had been told that he was fortunate to be alive. As the days passed this preyed on his mind. And when I was not there to see it, he started reading the Bible we had been given when we were married. Then he, knowing my parents were Christians, started asking me about death and life after death. Although I wasn't a believer, I remembered enough to tell him that he needed to be saved. I could tell him no more as I needed to be saved myself.

**I want to know it all**
In January, as Mark was still off work and walking with crutches, we went to Belfast to visit my mum and dad. 'Do you ever read the Bible you got when you were married?' Mum asked, on our last night there. 'Yes,' I answered, much to her surprise. Then it was Mark's turn to surprise them. 'Can I ask you something?' he said to my dad. 'What do you want to know?' Dad asked, sitting down opposite us. Mark thought for a minute before answering, 'I want to know it all.'

Dad told Mark about the Lord Jesus, who he was and what he came to earth to do. I had heard it all as a child, but Mark had not. He was hearing the gospel for the very first time. My dad's account of the Lord's death and resurrection were new to him. He listened as Dad shared his testimony, explaining that all he did was believe God's promise. 'For God so loved the world, that he gave his only begotten Son, that whosoever believeth in him should not perish, but have

37

everlasting life' (John 3:16). As Dad spoke on, he did a strange thing. Having been speaking directly to Mark, he turned his eyes and attention on me.

'Mark,' I asked, when Mum and Dad left the room later, 'did that make any difference to you?' 'Yes, it did,' he answered. 'I'm saved.' I knew before he told me. I knew because Dad had known, that was why he had turned from Mark to me. He had said all that was needed to my husband. In my heart I knew two things. I knew that Mark was right with God, and I knew I was not, and I needed to be.

I couldn't sleep at all that night. Sitting up through the small hours, I read and read the Bible. But nothing I read helped me. Knocking gently on my brother's door, I went in and sat on his bed. 'I want to be saved,' I said quietly. 'What can you tell me that I don't already know?' Instantly awake, he helped me see the way. I eventually fell asleep, telling the Lord in prayer that I was trusting him to save me. When I awoke in the morning I felt no different at all. It was 1st February, and we left Belfast for Peterborough. When I warned Mark that if there was no change in him by our wedding anniversary on 27th February, I had not the least anticipation how momentous a change there could, or would, be. That night, back in our own home, we read the Bible and talked about its message. For a week I struggled to be sure I was a Christian. We read. We talked. And I felt just exactly the same old me.

Going to church for the first time that Sunday was hard. We arranged to leave Scott with Mark's parents, though they nearly fell on the floor when we told them where we were going! Sneaking into the back of Whittlesey Baptist Church, we thought no-one would notice. But that would have been rather hard as Mark was still on crutches at the time. When the pastor asked us why we were there we didn't really give an answer. Our arrival was a real encouragement to the church people as they were praying for young families to come.

**Saved or not?**
Family and friends back in Belfast, delighted at the news of Mark's conversion, prayed for me. I decided to ask the pastor to visit us, and he came within the next few days. 'How do you know if you're saved?' I asked him as soon as he had sat down. 'Well, I'm not often asked that question,' he said. He talked for quite a while with me but I couldn't understand why he was so relaxed. There I was struggling with myself, and all he did was leave me a book called *All about Conversion*. But I read the book and it helped me a lot. I discovered that one of the evidences of being saved is that God changes your life. And he had certainly made changes in my life since we were in Belfast. I was partly reassured.

But a question still niggled in my mind. If God was making changes in my life, why did I not feel any different? I think I was waiting for flashing lights or some other such dramatic happening! Mark and I read the Bible and the pastor's book. In the New Testament I discovered that, while Paul had a dramatic conversion, Lydia's heart was opened in a very quiet way by the Lord. Timothy was different again. Because he was brought up by a Christian mother and his grandmother was a believer too, he knew the gospel from childhood. I learned that it doesn't matter when or how we are saved as long as we are saved. Some come through fiery experiences, some come through great floods of emotion, some are nearly drowned in life's sorrows, but all come through the saving blood of Jesus, shed at Calvary.

The truth of it came home to my heart. I was converted, we both were. I was saved, we both were. And we were both being changed. At last we had something in common. We had a foundation, Jesus Christ, on whom we could begin to build our lives and our marriage. God's hand had been in it all. It was he who had made me miss my plane. The times and the dates were all in his hands. What a relief. What an inexpressible relief to know that we were held in the hollow of the hands that made the universe.

In June 1991, when we were baptised in

Whittlesey Baptist Church, our pastor gave us each a card with a verse on it. Mine was the reply to the question that I first asked him. 'For it is by grace you have been saved, through faith – and this not from yourselves, it is the gift of God not by works, so that no-one can boast' (Ephesians 2:8-9). Pastor Brian Keen and his wife were a great help and support to us in the following two years. He was a real shepherd and friend, loved by everyone who knew him. We learned a lot through his ministry and valued his prayers. During that time we were blessed with our second son, Arron, who was brought into a very different home to the one Scott had come three years earlier.

### Back home to Belfast

From the time of his conversion, Mark wanted to live in Belfast. So, in 1991, when Arron was eighteen months old, we moved 'back home'. We felt the Lord leading us there. But we didn't forget those we left behind in England. And they didn't forget us. The people in our church in Whittlesey continued to remember us in prayer. We were sad when Brian died four years later. He and Hazel will always be dear to us.

It took us a while to settle in Belfast, but we knew it was right for us to be there. We both grew in the Lord, and I hope we are still growing. This was especially noticeable in Mark's life. It had been hard for him in his home town where his contemporaries refused to let him leave his past behind. The move to Belfast allowed him, allowed us, to start afresh. Mark, a roofer by trade, works in a small building firm. And we are both involved in the work of our congregation. I help in the Mothers' and Toddlers' Group and Mark is a deacon, and a leader in our Young People's Association.

Since making our home in the province, we have been blessed with two more children, Lois and Stephen. It is our hearts' desire to see them all converted while they are still young, before the world gets a hold of them, as it did of me. For I know from personal experience that anyone who chooses to be a friend of the world becomes an enemy of God.

# GHILLEAN PRANCE

Although I was born in Suffolk, my early childhood was in Dunvegan on the Isle of Skye and later in the Cotswolds, both in country areas where I was surrounded by natural beauty. I cannot remember when I was not fascinated by natural history and all living objects around me, whether butterflies, birds, sea urchins or plants, and I thought of it all as God's creation. An early recollection is of being severely reprimanded by my parents for picking a harebell on the way to Dunvegan Church. In those days that was not a thing to do on the Sabbath. However, as you will see, in the end that put me off neither botany nor the church!

When my family moved to Gloucestershire in 1946, when I was seven years old, I found myself in a country house with fifty acres of woodland surrounding it. What better place could there be for a budding botanist. My interest in plants delighted two of my elderly aunts who were both most knowledgeable amateur botanists themselves and patient teachers. They taught me how to collect and identify plants. Aunt Gertrude was a retired missionary who had spent most of her life in India. When she stayed with us church activities were very much part of the routine. As my father died when I was nine, and was an invalid for two years prior to his death from lung cancer, perhaps the influence of his two septuagenarian sisters was all the more important to my early life.

After an extremely unhappy experience in a prep school in Cheltenham, where I was a weekly boarder, I was able to persuade my nanny to plead with Mother for a transfer to another school. Mother was too preoccupied with my father's terminal illness to notice the evils of that school. I was fortunate to be transferred to a prep school in Malvern which specialised in sending pupils to Malvern College. And that is how I ended up at Malvern in 1953, and it was there that my interest in botany was fostered and developed.

## School, College and Christ

I feel that it was God's good pathway for my life that I found myself in the house of Bill Wilson, the biology master at Malvern College. He did so much to encourage me and other boys in his house who had an interest in natural history. On days off classes he would take us all over southern England looking for rare plants or birds or butterflies. And since he was so knowledgeable and enthusiastic Malvern really confirmed my desire to be a botanist and to work towards getting to university to study the subject.

During my time at Malvern I continued to attend and take part in the activities of the local village church, including acting in the many religious plays which my mother wrote for the church. School chapel and religion classes made me think about matters of faith and I read Emil Brunner's *Our Faith* and several books by C. S. Lewis such as *Mere Christianity* and *The Screwtape Letters*. But although this planted the seed of my faith, it was not a very important part of my life at that time. I never rebelled from the Christianity which was an important part of my mother's life. However, botany was certainly supreme then. In spite of only a moderate academic record, still catching up from the wasted years at that awful prep school, by doing well in their entrance exams and interviews I managed to gain a place at Oxford University to read botany. Again I feel that was part of the plan for my life.

I was really excited on arriving at Oxford in the autumn of 1957 to work for a degree that was pure botany and nothing else. However, a great surprise soon followed when I accepted the invitation to a freshman's tea offered by the Oxford Christian Union. As the atmosphere seemed so friendly I also accepted their invitation to attend evening service on my first Sunday in Oxford. I was quite amazed when I found myself taking most interest in the sermon, the part of services I usually found most boring! The preacher's words seemed to make good sense, for it was the first time that I heard the gospel of Jesus Christ so clearly expounded. Consequently I did not need invitations to go to the services in future weeks because I was anxious to hear more. It was on my third Sunday at Oxford that I accepted the preacher's invitation to go to the front of the church and be prayed for by a fellow student. More importantly, I accepted not just an invitation to leave my seat, but I accepted Christ as my personal Saviour. The joy and the release of the burden of sin was enormous, and this experience changed my life in many ways.

## A time of decision

Accepting Christ was not the only decision that I had to make in my new life. As I, with the help of members of the Christian Union, learned to study the Bible properly and to pray, my faith and commitment to Christ grew. One of the great strengths of the Christian Union was the way in which it provided teaching and counselling to young Christians. It was not long before I began to wonder what God's will for my future was, and how my botany and faith belonged together.

That first summer vacation found me as a team member of a beach mission in Frinton, Essex, along with other students, taking the Christian message to holiday-makers there. I enjoyed that experience and joined in the activities with considerable enthusiasm, even being allowed to speak at two of the morning beach services. It happened that I was one of the few people on the mission team with a car because my brother was abroad on holiday and had lent me his. One of my fellow-workers on the mission needed to be driven to Norwich to comfort her brother and sister-in-law who had just unexpectedly lost their newborn baby. The mission leader called me aside and asked if I would be willing to drive Anne Hay to Norwich. I was particularly glad to do this because I found Anne most lively and interesting. The result of the mission of mercy was that we fell in love, and I met my life partner. Three years later, when Anne completed her degree in English at London University, we were married.

The purpose of bringing Anne into the story at this point is to introduce her father, a retired missionary who was then the rector of a small central city church in Norwich. By the time I started visiting the Hay home as Anne's boy friend and later fiance, I was seeking God's will for my future, whether I should give up botany and volunteer for full time Christian service of some sort and was already exploring the pathway to become ordained in the Church of England. Mr. Hay was one of my main counsellors on this matter and he suggested gently that my knowledge and passion for plants was a God-given gift. He felt that I had not spent my life since early childhood learning so much about botany for no purpose, and that the church needed more truly committed laymen, especially some with a scientific background. After prayer, Bible study and much discussion with Mr. Hay and others, I knew God wanted me to continue studying botany and to make my career in that field. The Lord has certainly honoured that decision in all the opportunities I have had to witness to him in many different circumstances around the world. I feel as much a sense of calling to the pathway my life has taken as if I had been ordained or in any other form of professional Christian service.

**Amazonia**

I was married to Anne on 13th July 1961, at the beginning of my second year as a postgraduate student in the Oxford Forestry Department where I was working for a doctorate in tropical botany. By the beginning of my third and final year of doctoral studies I was offered, without having applied, the opportunity of two different jobs, one in Kenya and the other in New York. Africa was obviously the more appealing to a tropical botanist longing to get into the field to see the plants I was studying for my thesis.

However, I also enquired about the New York job because it was more closely linked to the subject of my thesis. In fact, it was to continue work on the *Chrysobalanaceae*, the plant family I was studying. When I asked about funds to travel to New York to take up that job, the head of science there replied that there were no funds available for that, but if I would join an expedition to Surinam in South America first he could pay my air fares from his expedition grant. As the chance of an expedition to Surinam, where I knew that many *Chrysobalanaceae* grew, was too good an opportunity to miss, my choice was the New York job. I know that was God's leading because, after a few months, the Kenya project folded up. I would have gone there just to be sent back home. A week after I passed my doctoral exam and our first child was born, I left for South America.

The Surinam expedition was led by a most accomplished field botanist, Howard Irwin. Because he was a good teacher the experience whetted my appetite for more tropical field work. I was in Brazil the following year, 1964, and before long was in charge of developing an Amazonian exploration programme for the New York Botanical Garden. For the following decade we lived alternate years in New York and Brazil. Anne bravely and somewhat reluctantly took up roots and moved back and forth with our children. The first time she accompanied me to Brazil we travelled with our two daughters, Rachel and Sarah, aged three years and ten weeks respectively.

During this time of intensive botanical exploration I had a wonderful time learning more about this part of God's creation, and how the various plants and animals interact. The expeditions collected over 350 new species of plants that had never before been discovered or named. The expedition programme grew and was highly successful, partly through the support of Anne, who always ran the headquarters in Manaus.

I became involved in Christian work in the Amazon on my second expedition because of the insistence of missionary friends, the Halsells in Belém, who had warmly welcomed me into their home on my first visit. Perhaps my eagerness to go to a small church in a mud hut on the outskirts of the city with Tom Halsell lessened a little when he informed me that I was speaking to his congregation that night and he was not translating! With my rudimentary Portuguese I just coped with giving a personal testimony. But Tom's insistence that it was time I started trying to speak about my faith in Portuguese got me launched. Since then I have spoken and preached in churches of many denominations in Brazil. When in Manaus, where the family lived, we enjoyed fellowship with both the Baptist and Presbyterian churches.

As I enthusiastically pursued my botanical career I had the opportunity of visiting many local churches and mission stations where it was most affirming to the believers to meet a scientist who was also a Christian. When we started attending the First Baptist Church in Manaus, the members found it hard to believe that we were not yet another missionary family, especially as we were introduced in the service as missionaries from The New York Botanical Garden Mission! Gradually they realised and appreciated that we were Christian lay people and, before long, Anne was teaching an adult Sunday school and I was involved in seminars for their university students who were having difficulty reconciling their faith with the science they were being taught.

My Amazon career took a significant change in direction after an evening in the home of the Director of the National Amazon Research Institute, the institution with which I was collaborating for all the field work. The Director, Dr. Paulo Machado, complained that he was desperate because he had just heard that two more researchers whom the Institute had trained abroad, and who promised to return to Manaus to work, had reneged on the commitment. One wrote to say that he was remaining in the United States, and the other that he was going to work in Rio de Janeiro where there were better research facilities and a better lifestyle. I casually suggested that he should set up a postgraduate course in Manaus where the Amazon forest was all around as a laboratory, suggesting that if the students trained there they would become so enthusiastic about the Amazon forest that they would never leave the region.

Dr. Paulo was a man of action, which is why he later became his country's Minister of Health. Announcing that the head of the National Research Council was coming through Manaus the next afternoon on his return from a trip to the USA, he asked if I would prepare an outline for such a course and give it to him the next morning! Rashly I agreed, although it was already after 9 pm, because it seemed a useful thing to do. Anne and I spent the whole night working on a complete MSc programme in tropical botany. As I outlined each unit of the course Anne wrote it in longhand. How I wished I had even one catalogue of a university course in the expedition equipment. Giving a full course outline to Dr. Paulo at 9 am, we collapsed into our hammocks for some rest.

Early in the afternoon Dr. Paulo sent for us, welcoming us with, 'Your course has been approved by the Research Council.' I replied that it was his course. He disagreed, insisting that I was to be the first Director in spite of my stressing that I had a job to do for the New York Botanical Garden. As the result of my rash suggestion of a course, Dr. Paulo travelled to New York where he persuaded the President of the Garden to loan me to INPA for two years to set it up. For the following two and a half years, while I did just that and saw the first group of eleven students through their degrees, Manaus was our family home. The course programme continues today in botany, ecology, ichthyology (fishes), entomology and forestry and, in 1998, it awarded its 100th PhD. The students from that first course have all remained in the Amazon region, and several are now heads of various departments working on the conservation of the forest. God's leading is sometimes unexpected. And at that point in our lives that was how it was for us.

## Environmental Destruction

One of the descriptions which I included in the course programme was environmental ecology, and I persuaded a colleague, Robert Goodland of The New York Botanical Garden, to teach it as he is an expert in environmental impact. He agreed, provided I could get funds to take the students to do a practical impact study of the then recently constructed Trans-Amazon highway. As I was able to get the Brazilian air force to fly us all there the course took place. The highway was built mainly as a means of settling colonisers from the drought-stricken northeast of Brazil. An elaborate plan was devised to allocate land and set up villages, towns and cities all along its length. It was an extremely controversial project because it opened up the Amazon rainforest and encouraged the settlers to cut the forest down to allow them to plant rice.

What we saw on that visit changed our lives. The settlement project was a disaster, and few of the farms produced any harvest at all. Some of the colonisers were already thinking of returning to their home states. The Trans-Amazon project never worked well and was eventually abandoned a few years later. Robert wrote a book about it entitled *Amazon Jungle: Green Hell to Red Desert?* I changed the emphasis of my research, becoming involved both in ways to conserve areas of forest, and ways in which to use the forest sustainably without causing the sort of destruction that we had witnessed along the highway. Ever since that experience I have been deeply engaged in environmental issues both at home and abroad. The destruction of the Amazon rainforest continues today. And in 1997, because of drought caused by the El Nino effect, many farmers' fires spread into the forest causing much damage. The students who joined Robert and me on that course were also deeply affected, many have continued to be strongly involved in environmental issues.

## God the Creator
My concern about environmental issues led me to a much closer integration of the two parts of

my life, my scientific career in botany and my Christian faith. As I began to see what the scriptures say about caring for God's creation, which is being so badly abused, I became involved with the Au Sable Institute for Environmental Studies. This Christian institute in Michigan, USA, seeks to teach about the environment to students from Christian colleges, universities and schools. The Institute also brings together, through a series of discussion meetings, many people who are wrestling with these issues. I co-ordinated one of these on the topic *Missionary Earthkeeping.* In it we discussed ways in which mission work can also do a lot for environmental protection.

I have become more deeply involved in the environment because of my faith rather than in spite of it. Although the Bible contains guidelines to the stewardship of God's creation, many Christians are fearful to become identified with environmental issues because of the New Age Movement, whose misguided adherents tend to worship creation rather than the Creator. But those of us who have accepted Christ as our personal Saviour clearly worship the Creator, marvelling at his revelation through the beauty of his creation.

'The LORD God made all kinds of trees grow out of the ground – trees that were pleasing to the eye and good for food' (Genesis 2: 9). I like that verse especially because it puts the aesthetic beauty of creation first and the utilitarian, the food, second. Yet we overuse the latter through greed, cutting down too much forest, fishing too many fish from the oceans and abusing the soil until it is no longer productive.

'God saw all that he had made, and it was very good' says Genesis 1:31. Yet his creation is being assaulted by humankind to such a great extent that pollution is ruining our land, atmosphere and oceans. Species are becoming extinct at an unprecedented rate; the protective layer of ozone in the stratosphere is breaking down and the climate is changing because of an increase in greenhouse gasses in the atmosphere. The existence of the good life which God created on planet Earth is seriously threatened. Christians who believe that God created the universe in which we live cannot remain complacent. The creed we say in my church affirms our belief in 'God the Father, Maker of heaven and earth and of all things visible and invisible.' If we believe this we must be called to action.

The most wonderful truth of all is that Christ was in creation. 'He (Christ) is the image of the invisible God, the firstborn over all creation. For by him all things were created: things in heaven and on earth, visible and invisible, whether thrones or powers or rulers or authorities; all things were created by him and for him. He is before all things, and in him all things hold together' (Colossians 1:15-17). 'In the past God spoke to our forefathers through the prophets at many times and in various ways, but in these last days he has spoken to us by his Son, whom he appointed heir of all things, and through whom he made the universe' (Hebrews 1:1-2).

I seek to serve God as a scientist Christian through helping to protect his creation, encouraging environmental stewardship by fellow believers in many churches, and by using the prominence I now have as Director of the Royal Botanic Gardens at Kew to speak out for Christ. When I do this in the media I often get letters of encouragement or thanks from Christians. For example, after mentioning my faith on *Desert Island Discs* I received quite a few. However, it is not just the believers I seek to reach, it is also those who do not yet have the joy that I have found in my personal relationship with the Saviour who died for my sins and the sins of the world.

Christ died for the whole of creation, to bring hope to the creation as well as to those that accept him as their Saviour. My faith in him leads me to testify to what he has done for me and to help to protect his creation which reveals my God's magnificence.

# MORWEN HIGHAM

Some people can remember a long way back in their childhood, but for me my sixth year stands out vividly. I was suddenly taken very ill, and a school friend of mine became ill at the same time. I got better as the months went by and eventually recovered, but my friend gradually got worse and worse until she died. It was my first experience of death and it frightened me. No-one had an answer to my questions or was able to console me in my distress.

My upbringing was a religious one as I was born into a family that feared God. But my religion did not answer the problems of life and death. We were a Welsh Calvinistic Methodist family and attended church regularly, learning many Bible verses each week, studying the *Rhodd Mam* which was a catechism, and really enjoying church activities. My maternal grandparents were the fruit of the 1904-05 Welsh Revival, devout and godly people. And my earliest memories were of a well-worn Bible always open on the kitchen table, and the Sabbath kept strictly. All preparations for Sunday meals and Sunday services were done on Saturday night: cleaning shoes, preparing vegetables, baking bread and cakes. We did not resent the tasks, taking it all as our ordinary way of life.

## An impressionable six year old

I can remember my aunt, my father's sister, coming to visit us. She had no religious background, though clean living and loving to us all. However, she had recently been converted and together with her husband had started to attend a Brethren Hall. She was very burdened for the souls of my parents and I recall hearing, as a very impressionable six year old, the sobbing of my aunt as she pleaded with my parents to come to Christ because he had died for them. She knew that when she died, she had an assurance of sins forgiven and hope of heaven. My mother's reaction was typical of that religious age. What cheek to suggest that she, a church organist for nineteen years and with her father an elder in the Presbyterian Church, was still unsaved! It was the discussion point at meal-times and in the evenings for months afterwards. Into my impressionable mind there came the certainty of a heaven and hell, and of the Being of God, who held the destiny of our souls in his hands. The fear of dying was underlined in my thinking. By that time we were living through the war years and the uncertainty of life was stressed upon us daily.

When I was twelve years old my father started to go blind, and the prospect of ill-health and the uncertainty of life struck us as a family. We began to realise that God was remote from us, we had no reality of his presence. Our religion gave us no comfort. My father wanted me to read the Bible to him, and also the hymn book. But Mother became angry with God and demanded, 'Why should this happen to us? What have we done to deserve this?' I began to take my father to the prayer meetings at church when I was about fifteen years old. Our minister thought I was seeking the Lord and he would ask me to give out a hymn, or to sing and pray. The hymns I chose would always be,

> Ni fethodd gweddi daer erioed
> A chyrraedd hyd y nef.
>
> (William Williams Pantycelin)

This translates:

An urgent prayer would never fail to reach heaven.

Or another

> Cyn i Dduw dy rhoi i fyny
> Cyn it orwedd yn y bedd
> Cyn i angau dy ddychrynu
> Myn adnabod Duw a'i hedd'
>
> (translated from a hymn by Charles Wesley)

Which translates

Before God gives you up,
Before you lie in the grave,
Before death frightens you,
Make sure you know God and his peace.

God was working in my heart and I had begun
on the quest for a purpose in life. The world and
all its pleasures were pulling one way and he,
through the circumstances of life in our home,
was pulling another. It was a strange duality.

**Religious or Christian?**
I started working in 1942 at the age of fifteen in
the Evacuation Department of the Local Rural
Council Offices. My father's blindness compelled
me to find work rather than go on with my
education. For three years my boss who was a
Christian witnessed to me, but I could not
understand what he said. However, listening to
discussions between him and another colleague
who was a Christadelphian[1] was quite challenging
and enlightening. By the age of eighteen my life
was one big struggle as the pull to go the way of
the world and to stop going to church was very
strong.

---

1. Christadelphians – a cult founded in 1848 by John
Thomas. Among other doctrines it teaches that Jesus
Christ is not God and that the Holy Spirit is a 'force' not
a person.

My religious parents thought that the way to keep me going to church was for me to become a member of the fellowship. The minister came to see me at their request and told me I was old enough to become a part of the church. When I replied in no uncertain terms that I was not converted, he assured me that not everyone needed to be converted. After all, he concluded, I had been brought up to attend all the services and knew scriptural verses and hymns. Eventually, to please my parents, I became a member of the Welsh Calvinistic Methodist church in my village. As I was partaking of Holy Communion for the first time the minister quoted the verse 'He that eateth and drinketh unworthily, eateth and drinketh damnation to himself' (1 Corinthians 11:29, AV). I became acutely conscious of my unworthiness and went home feeling very frightened. Then, falling on my knees, I sought God and prayed as I had never prayed before, 'Lord, show me what I need, for I don't know what I need.' It was a strange prayer, but an earnest prayer from the depth of my being.

After church on Sundays we would sit around the table discussing and arguing about Christianity, much to my mother's annoyance. I had been taught in Sunday School that I was a sinner, and I believed it, but I could not understand what MY sin was. I had never murdered nor lived an immoral life. I knew I was not perfect, but I was not aware of being sinful in the sight of God.

## Light dawns

Three months after my cry to God to show me what I needed, I was invited to a Youth for Christ rally in Llanelli. Because I had promised a school acquaintance that I would attend, I endeavoured to keep my word. The services were interesting, and there were so many young people around me, some of whom I had known from my school days. I listened intently to the testimony and the sermon, when the preacher spoke on 'Thou art weighed in the balances, and art found wanting' (Daniel 5:27, AV). During the preaching of the Word of God my eyes were opened for the first time to see my need of a Saviour. I realised that my sin was against him because I had not come up to the standard he demanded. Then I knew that even by one sin – not loving God with all my heart, soul, mind and strength – I was barred from heaven for eternity. My eyes were opened to see that the death of Christ on the cross was for sinners like myself. It was a remarkable experience to go into a meeting blind to my sin, arguing that I had lived a good, moral life; and to come out of that same meeting able to sing,

> My sin, oh the bliss of this glorious thought,
> My sin, not in part, but the whole,

Is nailed to his cross, and I bear it no more:
Praise the Lord, praise the Lord, O my soul.

(Horatius Gates Spafford)

Looking back now over those years I see that the good hand of God was on my life. There were still struggles to give up worldly pleasure and ungodly friends that would pull me down to their worldly ways. My own minister, hearing of my experience of God's grace, invited me for a meal with his family. I spent several hours there being interrogated about my beliefs, as he attempted to undermine my faith by pointing out so-called discrepancies between the Old and New Testaments. Leaving their home, having missed the last bus home, I walked over a mile under a starry, moonlit sky, groping with the questions and statements of this learned man. It was a dark night for my soul but, as I looked up into the starlit sky, God drew near and enveloped me in his love. I knew God was a reality and that Christ, his own Son, had shown mercy to me in saving me. Lines of hymns such as,

Tis mercy all! immense and free;
For, O my God, it found out me!

(Charles Wesley)

became a deep assurance to me.

How much I had to learn from the Word of God. I longed to know the Bible quickly, by instant knowledge, but I have had to learn patience in studying and learning, leaning on God in times of difficulty and knowing his constant care. God is a wonderful teacher, teaching through all the circumstances of life. Knowing that his hand is upon me, I am assured he will take me safely home to heaven. One of my favourite hymns clearly states my own experience of the grace of the Lord in my life,

> To Thee, Thou dying Lamb,
> I all things owe;
> All that I have and am,
> And all I know.
> All that I have is now no longer mine,
> And I am not my own; Lord, I am Thine
>
> How can I, Lord, withhold
> Life's brightest hour
> From Thee, or gathered gold,
> Or any power?
> Why should I keep one precious thing from Thee,
> When Thou hast given Thine own dear self for
> me?
> (Charles Edward Mudie)

## Saved to serve

There is nothing more worthwhile in this world than knowing God through Jesus Christ, and making him known to others. My desire was to go to serve him immediately, leaving behind the difficulty of witnessing in my own village, church and family. But that was not his way. After months of seeking God's will, of prayer and searching the Word of God for his guidance, I shared my desire with my family. They were antagonistic to the thought and made life very difficult. But, if God calls, no one can stand in his way. I applied for full time service and my application was accepted. My preparation for service as a 'Sister of the People' with the Forward Movement of the Presbyterian Church of Wales was to work for six months in the village of Trethomas, near Caerphilly, observing the needs there and entering into what was to be my work for the Lord. It was a time of much poverty, both material and spiritual. I saw the apathy and misery of those living without Christ, and visited many on their deathbeds facing eternity without him.

Two years at Ridgelands Bible College in Bexley in Kent followed. That proved a blessed time of preparation. During my time there, I began to see the need of my own heart for growth in the Christian life, for a prayer-life that was vibrant, for dealing with relationships with others which could be a hindrance to any work for God, and for making lifelong friendships with those going to serve him in the four corners of the world. My privilege was great indeed – yet with the privilege came responsibility.

My longing was to be in God's will, doing his

work, and I prayed one night that I was willing to go anywhere 'but please don't send me back to Llwynhendy.' That was my own village. All the people there knew me: my family, my church and the local people had given me a hard time. Yet that was where the Lord sent me, to a large housing estate containing thousands of new houses built to rehouse people from the poorer areas of Llanelli. The Welsh-speaking villagers resented the English speaking invasion of their area. But they were poor souls, many of whom had never heard the gospel. I was twenty-three years old and my task was to do church planting in a hard, rough district where there were literally thousands of children and young people. The days were different then; all you had to do was wait for the children to come out of school and hand out leaflets inviting them to a children's meeting. Two hundred came the first week and soon we had three hundred attending. A prayer meeting and Sunday services were started in a local school, and the Christians who lived in the area helped by praying and working to bring the gospel of Jesus Christ to those needy people.

## Lives lived for the Lord

It seemed that God had given me a lifetime's work to do, but there was a perplexing time ahead. I met a young man, Vernon Higham, who asked me to marry him. After months of seeking to know God's will though his Word and prayer, he led me to accept Vernon's proposal. We were married and entered a life of Christian ministry together. 'His way is perfect' (Psalm 18:30 AV) and 'His ways past finding out' (Romans 11:33 AV). God never wastes any experience in our lives, each being used by him to prepare us for his service.

Our lives in the ministry were in three different churches. The first, in an industrial town in South Wales, was in the Calvinistic Methodist denomination. After being there for about eighteen months we came to a time of crisis. Most people did not appreciate the preaching of the gospel of our glorious God, and showed us by their actions that they wanted us to go. We searched our hearts to know whether we should leave and go back to secular work. Had God called us to be together? Had he called us into Christian ministry? Were we on the right course? For us there was no going back. God had put us where we were, and there we would stay until he moved us on. We prayed for a key soul to be saved as a seal upon our work. Expecting one of the elders or deacons to be converted, we were blessed instead by the saving of the young widow who was the church's cleaner/caretaker. She was a choice soul, who witnessed for her Saviour to the entire congregation, and went around every house in the town selling Bibles and evangelical literature. She was our encouragement and the seal upon our call.

After three years of service God called us to a country church. Our first son was one year old when we moved and it was when we were in the country that our daughter was born. Our time there restored my faith in people and took away a bitterness in my heart that was the result of the hurt of rejection and the hardship of the work. Amy Carmichael said, 'He hath not travelled far, who hath no wound, no scar.' Two years after we went to that church a farmer visited us on our return from holiday. 'We've watched you for two years,' he told us, 'Now we'll listen.' And they did. What a challenge and encouragement it was to find seeking souls coming to faith in the time that was left to us there. When we left that place we loved, it was in obedience to God's call to minister to the people of Heath Church in Cardiff.

Vernon and I worked hard, seeking the fulfilment of the word, 'I have much people in this city' (Acts 18:10 AV), to the point that Vernon's health broke when I was pregnant with our third child, a boy. His life was in the balance, and I had to face the possibility of bringing up three small children alone. It was a time of learning to trust God in a new way. My husband's illness lasted for fifteen years. During that time God chose to call many members into a living relationship with him. Others were drawn to the church from the world and the congregation grew, this despite Vernon's poor health. From a small beginning of around sixty souls, God slowly added to the church, 'such as should be saved' (Acts 2:47 AV). What the Lord did among us was all to his glory.

We have laboured together in the ministry for forty-three years, thirty-seven of them in Heath. And the God who saved me when I was eighteen years old has kept me. I have proved his promise that he will never leave me nor forsake me.

> We praise him for all that is past
> And trust him for all that's to come.
>
> (Joseph Hart)

# JOEL EDWARDS

On a clear, crisp day in May 1960 a BOAC plane from Kingston, Jamaica, touched down on the Heathrow tarmac. It rolled adjacent to the distinctive Queen's building and came to a gentle stop. A plane load of trans-Atlantic travellers stepped out into the fraudulent sunshine to face the unknown in Great Britain. At eight years old, I was a fellow-pilgrim on this flight which seemed to last for days. Together with my two older sisters I filed apprehensively to the waiting building to endure the mysterious process of being welcomed to the 'Mother Country', before emerging into the waiting arms of our mother and other relatives.

That day was precipitated by the sudden disappearance of our mother, who had fled the domestic tension of our home in Kingston and emigrated to England some two years earlier. Even at the tender age of six, my memories of home were a curious combination of childhood pleasures and the horror of waking early to the cries of an abused mother. Fatherhood was a concept rather than an experience, and even now positive recollections of a father-son relationship during those early years are few and far between.

But at the heart of my embroidered childhood recollections – school days and passing friendships – were the deep impressions of Elder Shaw and Newton Church in Kingston. Elder Shaw was a respected and revered, charismatic and inspirational preacher. He preached with a passion which not only kept me awake, but which also convinced me that he believed what he preached. At that age his words were unimportant to me, but his enthusiasm was infectious. It seems that I was not alone in my admiration of Elder Shaw's preaching, because the building was always filled with people caught up in responsive worship to the preaching of the Word.

## Different – but why?
In Jamaica, I was just a boy. In England I became a 'coloured person'. How strange! So genuine was the depth of my confusion that I was totally convinced that coloured televisions were special issues for 'coloured folk'! The matter of being different was never discussed or dealt with in any meaningful way. Although it was the fabric of one's existence as a black person in those pre-Black Consciousness days, a whole generation of black and immigrant people were given no tools of awareness with which to preserve themselves. The eroding impact of 'differentness'

was silently unrelenting. Never explained, it never made sense.

While it was never actually said aloud, I became convinced that to be different was probably the same thing as being daft. Normality meant being abnormal and developing two distinct lifestyles which never met in conscious dialogue. The truly Caribbean boy stayed at home and in church within the security of all that was familiar and affirming. The 'coloured' boy ventured out to school, always on the lookout to assimilate acceptable behaviour which would allow him the luxury of social and cultural conformity. It was hard to be critical of a world I did not fully understand. The fact that I only ever entered the home of my other 'coloured' friend and never even passed through the door of my white friend's home, was always an unquestioned mystery.

I think I was ten or eleven when I became a Christian. I know I was still in primary school and that the event took place during a convention in Handsworth, Birmingham. A pre-motorway trip from our home in London to Birmingham around 1962 was a major expedition. It started before sunrise and felt longer than the five-day event itself. If children survived the hazards of adult rectitude, conventions were fun.

## The last one's a monkey

At the convention I met up with a new friend called Bunnie. I imagine Bunnie was a nickname he acquired for his bright dancing eyes, his mischievous grin and his furtiveness; it seemed an excellent association of ideas. We were inseparable until the time we sat together in the front row of the meeting and listened with amusement to the altar invitation. 'The last one to the altar is a monkey,' said Bunnie. There was to be a count of three before the race to the altar began. As I did not want to be a monkey I set off in great haste on the count of three. On arriving at the rail, I looked to either side and then over my shoulder, only to see Bunnie doubled in hysterical laughter. Disappointed and cheated I felt there was nothing for it but to assume the position and appear to pray. I would settle things with Bunnie later.

I cannot describe clearly what happened next. What I do remember is that I was overwhelmed by a terrible sense of sin, and simultaneously by an even greater degree of forgiveness. I have no idea how hard or how long I cried. It seemed that my awful awareness of sin was compensated for by a special facility of repentance and a limitless supply of grace. When I stood, I felt freer than was possible to describe, and cleaner than I have ever known. I never saw Bunnie again.

**Failure and faithfulness**

It was not long before secondary school came along. My education at Sir William Collins Secondary School, near Camden in North London, represented a significant block of life-experience between the ages of eleven and nineteen. As it never occurred to me to consider doing my 'A' Levels at Sixth Form College, I remained in my third sixth year and had to run the gauntlet of jokes about becoming a grandfather while still at school! The madness of teenage years during this period was a bittersweet experience. Many of my negative perceptions about myself persisted, amongst them the growing recognition of what it meant to be poor. The final ignominy was to stand in the free-dinner line well into sixth form, and to suffer the silent shame of collecting the grant for free school uniforms from the 'special shop' in Tottenham Court Road.

It became evident that there was one way to make money and a name for myself, and that was stealing. Woolworths, and other shops with accessible stationery materials, developed a particular attraction for me. It was an ideal business: steal from the rich and sell to the poor – usually pupils in the junior school. My school experience, which was held in a watertight compartment of secular morality, rapidly distanced me from the coexisting spirituality which belonged to the church. The inevitable happened one day when I was 'shopping' in Woolworths and a low key, high impact arrest was made. In the stillness of my cell I realised that it was necessary for my behaviour and my experience of God to meet each day. The realisation of my frail vulnerability was a great and cleansing experience. Forgiveness and renewal came to me like rays of sunshine on a cloudy day. Despite my failure, I found God to be utterly faithful.

So consuming was my passion for the Lord over the years that followed that I was unaware how unusual my behaviour was. I only noticed that other teenagers seldom showed up where I was! But my concern was not to compare my devotion to God with other people, it was simply that being in God's presence gave meaning to my life. I was learning that being with God is even more important that doing things for God. But God did call me to do things for him, and our two youth leaders, Ron Brown and Miss McKenzie, made sure I did them!

**Answered prayer**
In 1971, when I was nineteen years old, I had a life-changing experience of the Holy Spirit. It happened during a period of unparalleled frustration and impatience. I felt my hunger for God had become so intolerable that I would die.

My prayers in that period were no more than staccato utterances which punctuated my deep dissatisfaction. The previous day, while walking under a bright blue sky, I had prayed, 'Lord, if you don't help me, I've had it!' And he did, wonderfully and gloriously!

When I stood to preach my first mini-sermon some weeks later, I was not prepared for the outflow which overtook me. My theme was the Lord's second coming. If I were to preach that same sermon again today, I would wish to review many points in the content, but I will always cherish the sense of God's presence that accompanied me in the pulpit.

## A series of shocks

A year earlier my plans to do a degree in sociology collapsed and, although I was not an academic student, my desire to go on to further studies did not desert me with my disappointing grades. When my pastor, Rudolf Kennedy, told me about a new degree in theology at a Bible College north of London, I wondered if this might be for me. A short time later I went, accompanied by my friend Carol, to London Bible College for an interview and was accepted as a student there.

Life at London Bible College was a culture shock, in fact, it was a series of shocks. It involved leaving home for the first time, discovering how insular my church experience had been, and coming to the awareness that others outside of my own tradition could *possibly* get to heaven after all, and that women wearing cosmetics and jewellery could conceivably be Christians! But perhaps my greatest shock came when I realised that I wasn't English. No-one had ever told me otherwise. This led me to take a few tentative steps further in self-discovery. And the conclusion? I knew for sure that I was a black person who belonged to Britain. But I was not an Englishman.

## On probation

My intention, on leaving LBC, was to head for the Probation Service, thus fulfilling a private goal I had cherished since sixth form. My application to the Middlesex Probation Service for the post of an ancillary worker led to an interview in the Tottenham office. 'I wouldn't have thought that a degree in theology was very relevant for work as an ancillary worker,' the main interviewer said. 'I would have thought so,' was my off-the-cuff response. 'The Bible is, after all, very concerned about people and I can think of no better preparation for dealing with human relationships than the study of the Bible.' I got the job!

Eighteen months as an ancillary worker seemed a long sentence, but it provided an excellent and well-used path to social work training at Middlesex Polytechnic, and eventual employment, in 1978, with the Inner London Probation and After-Care Service. I learned a lot about my own humanity as I did my job. So close was my social affinity to many of my North London clients that I felt I counselled myself through their situations! That tough time was lightened by the fact that I wasn't on my own. Carol and I had married in 1976. My wife, whose character is marked by undemanding faithfulness and a single-minded commitment to God, was a great support. Our son was born two years into our marriage.

In the same year I started work as a Probation Officer I began teaching our denominational evening Bible classes – the Ebenezer Bible Institute. And a year later I was appointed co-ordinator of the programme with full responsibilities for a hundred evening students and eight staff, including my own minister! What was truly amazing was that this was given to me although I was not a licensed minister within my church. It was a gesture of trust that I greatly appreciated. That work lasted for five years, and taught me the importance of a teaching ministry in the local church. It was during that time that our daughter was born.

## Changes

One evening, during an EBI staff meeting in our home, our national bishop, Selwyn Arnold, phoned to invite me to pastor a small church in Mile End, East London. I was in a state of shock for a week before I felt sufficiently sure of God's will to accept the invitation. Then followed one of the most painful experiences of my life – leaving the congregation that had been my spiritual home for twenty-five years, and the people to whom I owed much over that time of apprenticeship. But it had to be done. On 1st September 1985, we moved to our new congregation. The inaugural morning service went by me as if it were happening to someone else. Reality came at the end of the evening service when Amos Guthrie, one of the deacons, handed me a set of keys for the church buildings.

Our first five years were both novel and exciting, with all of the challenges and horrors of the learning experience. A new building and a growing church, together with a wider ministry and a full-time job as a probation officer, made life very difficult. It became evident that something had to go. Surrendering my work at EBI had simply not been enough. Added to that, the old restless feeling was upon me once again. Light dawned on me during dictation with my secretary one day. Laura had always viewed my hectic lifestyle with incredulity. That day, as we discussed holidays, she said, 'You take your holidays and go on those Christian things, don't you!' She was right. I took a bold step, changed to part-time work, and became the first male job-share probation officer in Holloway Women's Prison. It was hard work but, more than ever, I developed a deep appreciation for concepts like justice and mercy.

## And more changes

About that time, at Spring Harvest in 1987, I met Philip Mohabir, a man with an enormous heart for reconciliation. Philip told me about his burden to see reconciliation between estranged black churches and the wider evangelical church. He explained how this shared vision between senior black Christians and the Evangelical Alliance had led him to launch the West Indian Evangelical Alliance (now the African and Caribbean Evangelical Alliance). His relentless persuasion over a number of months resonated with my growing sense of direction, and eventually, in March the following year, I left my job-share post to become WIEA's General Secretary.

It was only then that events of earlier years began to fall into perspective. In providing a reconciliatory ministry between black and white Christians in the UK, my journey into the black church experience became bound up with my own experience and self-discovery. In an effort to get other Christians to understand the black experience of redemption, I grew to understand more fully many of the things I had felt intuitively in my early years. My work in my local church and within WIEA and the Evangelical Alliance became absorbing. I actually felt as though I now *understood* what I was about.

## Evangelical Alliance

In my fortieth year I was privileged to be ordained to the ministry – and our local church sent Carol and me on a weekend trip to Paris! One day, not long afterwards, I was arrested by what I can only describe as a divine cross-examination. The point was this: would I be willing to serve God should he take away all the things I enjoyed? I was forced to examine my motives deeply. It was shortly after that piercing experience that the old, now familiar, restlessness began to gather momentum again. But it hardly made sense because everything seemed to be going so well. But within a few weeks I understood. The Evangelical Alliance was undergoing restructuring and I was invited to consider a central role on the new and emerging Senior Management Team. The General Director, Clive Calver, asked me to give it prayerful thought. The following day, while still in a haze, I discussed it with the Vice-President of ACEA, Melvin Powell, and was given a gentle nudge. I found it hard to be convinced but, as in previous situations, my restlessness calmed as I became increasingly willing to say 'yes'.

Having had God's will confirmed in a most remarkable way, I finally agreed to accept the challenge. What was left of my restlessness gave way to apprehension as I found myself undertaking the task of co-ordinating evangelical initiatives within the UK across a broad variety of groups and individuals. The learning process began all over again.

## My God, my Guide

Since that time I have stood amazed at God's goodness as he has allowed me to assume even more responsibilities as a Christian leader. In early 1997 Clive Calver left the Evangelical Alliance to become the President of World Relief in America. I was thrilled to be appointed as his successor, beginning my new role as the General Director of the Alliance on the 1st June 1997. Over the past two years, it has been a pleasure to learn and to serve at such an exciting time in history.

My personal pilgrimage has not been spectacular. My experience is that God's guidance often makes more sense in retrospect. But, although we are wise after events, God is wise before them. He it is who knows the end from the beginning. We are told that David, the psalmist, 'served God's purposes in his generation' (Acts 13:36). That was hardly evident before or during the vicissitudes of his long life. But somehow, all the successes, failures and sins of David's life, failed to derail him from the fixed points of God's plan for him. His whole life conspired to serve a greater purpose, one which became much clearer in retrospect.

# CHRISTOPHER IDLE

If going to church could get you to heaven, I might be in with a chance. I have enjoyed church services of all sorts since my boyhood in Bromley, a Kentish town now engulfed by London's concrete. Like my brother David and sister Audrey, I attended Sunday School. Even better were the Church of England Prayer Book services of the 1940s and 50s, with good attendance, quality music, and resonant prayers. I decided I could never be a clergyman, being unable to say 'unfeignedly', which came twice every Sunday. Did candidates have special training against such pitfalls?

By the age of twelve that conviction wavered. I took Confirmation and Communion seriously, and began to think there might be room for me in spite of my stammer. Tensions at home at that time made my stammer worse. I still trip over words when speaking impromptu in gatherings of more than about three. Our parents were involved with church; they had met in a church youth fellowship. My mother maintained her lifelong loyalty, public and private, with a preference for dignity and a suspicion of 'nonconformists'. My father resumed his attendance in retirement. Whatever happened later, I remain deeply grateful for the eighty years of loving generosity that both of them gave me.

## School days

When at eight years old I entered Eltham College, I found myself firmly among free churchmen as this was a Congregational foundation originally for missionaries' sons. Eric Liddell had been a pupil, revered in his old school long before the film *Chariots of Fire*. Among the benefits of ten years at Eltham were a growing love of English literature, and *Congregational Praise* at daily Chapel. This book was rich in the work of Isaac Watts, whose hymns stirred me deeply. Secretly I feared I might become a prefect and have to read the Bible in chapel because I knew that was beyond me. My worries were unfounded. Although I enjoyed sport, I never summoned enough enthusiasm for rugby, or cricketing skills, to enter the set from which prefects usually came. Later my confidence in the Bible as the Word of God made me love to read and preach it.

In schoolboy debate I would support orthodox Christianity, sometimes with insufferable piousness, without fully understanding it. Theory and practice were far apart. But around my mid-teens two things happened, though I cannot now say which came first or how they mingled. I started to rethink my inherited attitude to war and peace, having previously strongly argued against the pacifism of a Quaker schoolmate. 'What about Hitler?' seemed a smarter question than 'What about Jesus?'. But a slim volume, deep in a bookcase at home, made me wonder if he was right.

## Coming to faith

By this time other friends were showing signs (as I now recognise) of authentic Christian conversion. Mike and Tony exhibited a commitment to living out their faith that was positively unsettling. Whatever my own state of heart, I knew the real thing when I saw it; beside their enthusiasm for Christ, my own version was a flimsy shadow.

I sometimes wish I could go on to describe my own dramatic repentance. But it was not like that. Having overcome suspicions of the brash, new Billy Graham crusade at Harringay in 1954, I attended and heard the evangelist explain Pharaoh's confrontation with Moses, and God. No goodness of ours, he said, outweighs our sin, which is dealt with only by Christ's death for us – for me. But Pharaoh hardened his heart! I did not get up out of my seat. I simply thought, 'This is what I believe too!' All my churchgoing had not brought home the stark reality of judgement and salvation. But I never had any doubts about the reality of sin; any 'belief' with no answer to that stood no chance with me. Something similar happened on a Christian teenage 'camp' in Devon. Although I did not understand the culture and language of that world, I did want to know more of what these young men ('officers') were urging on us.

Revelling in my sixth form days, I struggled with Latin, enjoyed Greek, and loved English. I wrote light-hearted pieces for enjoyment; words were always exciting. While many contemporaries went straight from school to university I decided to face the conscription issue first. An office job while I waited for 'call up' had one bonus; I worked close to All Souls' Langham Place, appreciating the lunch hour ministry of its young Rector, John Stott. By then I knew, unfeignedly, both whose side I was on and why.

## Conscientious objection

Six months on I was duly summoned, registered as a conscientious objector, and faced my tribunal. I had been well-briefed by older friends. Eighteen-year-olds who showed how pacifism actually worked were told that their objection was political, not moral; those who stuck to morality were informed that they were hopelessly impractical. Somehow I convinced them that I had weighed the issues, and was assigned to two years 'alternative service'.

For this, one category was 'food distribution' which provided a local job, stacking grocery shelves. Here was an eye-opener for a studious, young, middle class Christian, who was idealistic enough to see that he was hardly saving humanity by taking his six pounds a week from Bromley High Street. I looked elsewhere, and after being sacked from one job (sometimes a useful experience) I settled down to portering at Grove Park Hospital, a two-mile bike ride from home. This was not the world's toughest job. In a small hospital specialising in TB, the porters' mess was an extended card school and canteen with occasional breaks for work. Though I was the odd one out, and spent much of the 'on call' time reading books ('War and Peace' was one) I reached some level of acceptance among older workmates. My Christian faith was the topic of good-natured banter, some serious argument, but no great persecution. Like the shop, this was also a useful training-ground.

**Introducing Marjorie**
I also discovered a Nurses' Christian Fellowship (NCF), nominally open to everyone from porter to consultant. In practice it comprised mainly nursing staff; a male orderly expressing interest (Michael Wilcock – another 'conchie') was apparently barred because they met in the man-free zone of the Nurses' Home. Somehow I

evaded the ban, and joined for the first time a regular Bible study group. In those days it was mainly the Authorised (King James) Version, 'thee' and 'thou'; but I was struck by the seriousness with which everyone took each word. These older, wiser Christians showed great forbearance to a newcomer who thought he knew more than he actually did.

One nurse in particular interested me, though night duty meant that she missed my first few meetings. Nurse Rycroft's Christian name, I discovered, was Marjorie; we chatted when our paths crossed around the dustbins or meal-trolleys; even more when I was promoted to Hospital Messenger, for 4/- (20p) a week extra. Marjorie came from committed Brethren stock, but felt a need to move on, usually in an Anglican direction, while I was impressed by the simplicity of her Assembly. But the NCF led me unexpectedly back to the Church of England in the shape of Stanley Pert, evangelical Vicar of Christ Church, Bromley. He pointed me to the 39 Articles of Religion to see what the C of E really believed about the Bible, atonement and justification. To me this was meat and drink; give or take the forms of expression, here was the gospel. In the Church of England!

**And so to Oxford**

My hospital service completed, I went up to
Oxford in 1959. The Christian Union (OICCU)
had a lively group in my college, St. Peter's,
which immediately took me under its wing. They
marched us 'freshers' along to the North Gate
Hall for Saturday Bible Readings, St. Ebbe's
Church on Sunday mornings, and the evening
evangelistic Sermon. Although I resisted being
typecast (with my CND badge I was an OICCU
rarity) I joined in readily; a new world was
opening up. Speakers, prayer meetings, Inter
Varsity Fellowship and Banner of Truth books,
the exploring of doctrines and expectation of
conversions – all these were fresh delights.

I managed to combine OICCU's hectic
lifestyle (including the Daily Prayer Meeting)
with CND and study. Mercifully I had a
demanding tutor for my English course! Did he
ever discover that I spent part of my first vacation
behind bars, after one of the first mass sit-downs
at a Northamptonshire nuclear rocket-base?
Looking back, I might have spent more time
enjoying footpaths or football; two games in three
years seems now a tragic waste of mediocre
talent.

Marjorie and I were now clear about our love,
and marriage. Engaged in 1960, we prepared to
wait three more years before marrying. I was also
clearer about ministry. Students have many ways

of testing their perceptions of God's call; one landmark was London's annual 'Islington Week'. That was my first short taste of inner-city realities and I sensed I might be back. Next came theology at Clifton Theological College, Bristol, which later merged with Tyndale Hall and Dalton House, the women's college. Marjorie joined Dalton House on a year's course for wives and fiancees of ordinands. She too revelled in the opportunity for consistent Bible and pastoral studies.

## Marriage and ministry

We were married at what had become her church, Christ Church, Bexleyheath. A shared flat in Redland was our first home together. Marjorie resumed nursing until the following year when Timothy was born. Then the search began for a curacy. Our first appointment fell through, but St. Mark's, Barrow in Furness took us on and I was ordained in Cumbria, July 1965. My ordination text was Jeremiah 23:28, where the Lord says, 'Let him who has my word speak my word faithfully.' Jonathan was born soon after we arrived in Barrow, and his birth was an eventful beginning to our time there. We look back on St. Mark's with affection.

## Grief and relief

We then had no telephone. It was during one call-box contact with brother David that he broke the shattering news that Dad had just walked out. Shattering? Yes, and no. Looking back, we could have seen it coming. Dad had simply chosen his moment. It left Mum, David and Audrey to cope differently, with David handling most of the business. It also meant relief. We had grown up in a parental cold war. When Dad took his frequent evenings out and weekends away with a friend things were easier. I never thought this odd until I noticed how other fathers behaved. Dad's friend was a woman from wartime days in North Wales and he came to prefer her company to anything home could offer. We tacitly accepted this. It was the way things were. Neither as children nor as adults did we relate to the 'companion' with whom he now set up home in Hertfordshire, with one eye on retirement.

## The beginnings of hymn writing

But I had work to do; my first long-suffering Vicar was Willam Kelly – scholar, preacher, pastor, evangelist. Here my first hymns were written, as told in the collection *Light upon the River* (St. Matthias Press 1998). Bill never settled in Barrow and, when he moved nearer his West Cumbrian roots, I enjoyed holding the fort for six months until a new vicar arrived. Then came our next move. Jeremy had joined our family by now.

We needed to be nearer both Mum and Mum-in-Law. Marjorie's widowed mother would soon be on her own, as brother John and family were leaving for South Africa. My anonymous personal advert in the *Church of England Newspaper* produced two replies, one of which was from Eustace Davis, a former China missionary, Vicar of Christ Church Old Kent Road, in south east London. There was no house, he explained, and no salary. He doubted whether we would want to bring up our family there. We read his letter, and said to each other, 'This is it!' On one exploratory visit I was carrying a children's tent for our boys; 'I'm glad you've got that,' said Eustace, 'you might need it!'

**Back to stacking shelves!**
After much negotiation with church and state, we moved into an old shop in Asylum Road. The front counter became my desk and the grocery shelves our bookcases; I was a shelf loader again! Our first Sunday saw twenty people in Church both morning and evening even though torrential rain had put most of Lewisham under water. David and Mum got through the floods to join us. Eighteen months later we moved down the road, as Southwark Council wanted to demolish our 'shop'. Needless to say it still stands.

Christ Church taught me much. Tower blocks were new to us, and fairly new to Peckham; another four went up during our time. Marcus was born in 1970, in the Christian maternity hospital where Marjorie had trained as a midwife, still with the remarkable Doris Hawkins as Matron. Surrounded by sons, I was now more at ease with Family Services and children's groups. Some Sundays we taught as many as eighty children. Even more exciting for the gospel, and sometimes for our survival, was an open youth club reaching some of the early skinheads.

Six years on from ordination we felt the pressure of space and the need to move again. This proved quite close as the crow flies; over (or under) the Thames to St. Matthias' Poplar, the heart of East London. Our five years there were marked by more discoveries of God's grace, my first experience of a Church School (where I was Vicar, Governor and parent) and of church strife. God blessed us with a lively youth group – nearly all lads – and the testing initiative of a church-based street corner cafe. But a tiny group of 'charismatic' members seemed to recognise little authority but their own, and my response was not always the wisest. Before arriving I had been warned that our small parish was doomed to merge; in current jargon it was non-viable. We disagreed, with supporting statistics, but eventually accepted the inevitable since God was opening another door. The next door parish of Limehouse needed a Rector.

## Run down and built up
The first time Marjorie and I peeped into St. Anne's, I was sure it was not for us. Vast in proportions, infested with pigeons, disfigured by two hundred broken windows, ornamented with the tatty remains of a failed merger with an extreme high church; set against all that a small but hopeful congregation lost in the architecture – and a magnificent organ. But God had his plans and no-one else wanted the job! A reluctant Archdeacon and an enterprising Bishop (Trevor Huddleston) eventually agreed and our Poplar congregation joined the Limehouse remnant in October 1976. Marjorie has told some of our Limehouse story in *Joy in the City* (Kingsway, reprinted 1995), including flood, fire, thefts and break-ins – with God's mercy over every setback, and the gospel breaking in too. My appreciation of his sovereign grace grew through two eye operations. One came just after our regular prayers for healing. Our delayed arrival at Moorfields Eye Hospital might not have pleased my doctor, but as hands were laid on me that Sunday evening, our Father's hand was on us all.

After my father's 'partner' died, we visited his bungalow for the first time. Mum was by now contentedly settled in a residential home close to her beloved common. But in 1984, within the space of three months, we found ourselves arranging both their funerals. Dad's presence at Mum's was the first family reunion in twenty years. Then he too collapsed and died during some days away. Between the two came my second eye operation. The order and the timing were so clearly in a heavenly Father's hands, steering events which were totally outside our control. Marjorie's mother was perhaps the best-prepared for her passing two years later; facing cancer with courageous realism, she ended her earthly days peacefully at St. Christopher's Hospice. Soon afterwards Marcus left school. With no other ties to London we closed our two decades in the capital.

## A change of place and a change of pace

Then came six and a half totally different, fully absorbing Suffolk years, when I was Rector of seven small villages on the Norfolk border. Scenery, sky, homes, voices, lifestyles were all different; so were church meetings, community expectations, and travelling – we now had a car. Everything changed except the human heart and the gospel of redeeming love. I shelved many good things to give the parishes priority; the Proclamation Trust was not one of them. Pioneered by Dick Lucas, this had championed the cause of expository Bible preaching in town and country, and the better training of the preachers, young or old; this I still needed.

## Through troubled waters

We had hoped to stay in rural East Anglia until retirement. Our move back to the Old Kent Road was not due to boredom with Suffolk or fascination with SE London. The Church of England was sold on the idea of gender equality and it had begun to ordain 'women priests'. At my interview I had made clear where I stood, but pressure was applied everywhere to fit in with the new orthodoxy. The spinners and fixers were at work. Before the crucial Synod vote, opponents were labelled 'heretic' or 'blasphemer'. Afterwards we were urged at all costs to stay on board and leave old arguments behind.

I found all this logically incredible and personally draining; with other negative factors concerned often with fund-raising, we now planned one further move. I resigned without claiming the offered compensation; the cheapest housing was in the neighbourhood we knew already, and 1995 found us back in Peckham where we now live.

## Looking back

Four factors have, over the last sixty years, sustained my faith. First, whoever could have invented the gospel? Of course no-one could make the story up, or imagine such a Saviour as Jesus; but I am also struck by the extraordinary divine imprint on the truth that we are justified – counted right before God – by his grace, through faith alone. Many ideas, philosophies, even Christian insights are relevant in some situations, powerless in others. The gospel, striking fatally at all self-righteousness as it did with mine, has proved relevant to every person, in every time, place, mood or need.

Then, for most of them, comes the love, loyalty and prayerfulness of Marjorie. The amazing strength which God gives through prayer together, morning, evening and countless special occasions, are beyond price. I admire single and widowed clergy but I cannot envisage how they cope with some extremes of Christian ministry.

Next, in spite of the appalling faults of the church, including those I share, the personal, doctrinal, and structural flaws, not least (though not only!) in the Church of England – I still find far less hypocrisy in the church than outside it. The critic whose only answer to anything the church says or does is to cry 'hypocrite' is in terminal self-delusion. For denying the evidence, unbelievers are hard to beat; only Christians have the resources to face the facts of life and death – and the heights of love and joy.

And though I am not a seeker for signs and wonders, some of the most potent corroborations

I have seen are those of perfect timing by the sovereign God – ultimate authority and ultimate love. Clearly and personally, the Lord Jesus Christ expresses his very nature; there is none like him, no people like his.

# MARIE-CHRISTINE LUX

How comforting it is to be reminded that God
has not finished with us, that he will complete
what he has undertaken in our hearts and in our
lives, and that with him, nothing is impossible:
'He who began a good work in you will carry it
on to completion until the day of Christ Jesus'
(Phil. 1:6).

Who would have dreamed that a child born of
Belgian parents in the very southern part of the
then Belgian Congo would one day be at this end
of the pen, telling you how God worked in the
most exquisite and special way in her life? Were
I given only one word to summarise it, I would
choose Ebenezer ('Thus far has the Lord helped
us', 1 Sam. 7:12). Mine was a very nominal
Roman Catholic background, where the name of
God was never mentioned and church was only
the place you went to for a baby's christening
(that included mine!), a wedding or a burial. I
had the happiest childhood I could ever have
wished. Born a tomboy, I relished the constant

outdoor activities offered to us in the tropics, climbing trees (mango trees were best for that purpose!) while playing cowboys and Indians or Second World War resistance games. Where we got our ideas from is hard to tell. We didn't have television, but we had vivid imaginations. There were few toys but nature around us provided the perfect tools and we moulded and shaped them to fit our purposes.

**Mud between my toes**

School was also a pleasant experience but what I remember most fondly were my 'expeditions' there and back by foot, in torrential rain, well protected under a thick plastic cape. Shoes in hand, I waded in the gutters overflowing with rapid flowing muddy water. How I loved the sensation of thick mud making its way between my toes. School, however, faded into insignificance compared to the sports activities we had every day. Classes started at 7am and usually finished at 1pm and after that life started for real. Mum picked my sister and me up at school, then we joined Dad at the Olympic Swimming Pool for at least one hour of fun in the water before diving into the egg sandwiches she had prepared for her ravenous family. Then it was either hockey, tennis, ballet classes or judo depending on the day of the week. That was followed by more fun and games, especially with the boys of my age, then home at last to do school work. What a life indeed!

At Independence, the Congo became Zaire. Seven years later, when I was fourteen years old, my parents decided it wasn't safe to stay there and the standard of schooling was declining quite rapidly. I couldn't accept being torn from what I loved so dearly, especially as everything changed so drastically. It was like passing from daylight into the darkest of night, like entering a tunnel with no exit and no headlights on either. I simply wasn't prepared for it.

## Why? Why? Why?

From tropical Zaire I was plunged into a very wet, grey and cold Belgium. Our mixed school was exchanged for an all-girls State school where girls of my age were already into petticoats, make-up and boyfriends. Little wonder they tended to ignore this kid who still wanted to play marbles and run everywhere. There were no more trees to climb. The playground was all grey and hard concrete like the country we now lived in. A quiet and resolute rebellion set in. Why had we to leave Zaire? Why didn't my parents leave me there? Why? Why? Why? I determined to work hard at school for fear of having to repeat grades, aiming, as I was, to escape as soon as I was of age to do so. Then I fully intended to go back to where I felt I belonged. I had no idea that what I traced for myself in my imagination was quite different from the plans my Maker had. My deep unhappiness made me long for something, who or what I did not know. But it made me start seeking.

Secondary school came and went, fairly turbulently in my inner being but uneventfully. I chose to study tourism, despite good grades, because it was the shortest course of further education studies. Before the age of twenty-one, I had the qualifications to work as a travel agent. But no-one wanted to employ such a young and inexperienced person. I decided to travel and gain experience, thinking that would equip me to be a good advisor to tourists. The easiest way to do this was to join the Merchant Navy for a year, then to emigrate to Australia.

## Life on the ocean wave

While at sea, there were plenty of opportunities to watch the ever changing oceans, and to admire the night sky which resembled a pure black velvet cloth sparkling with millions of tiny fragments of shiny diamonds. Surely Someone had to be responsible for such awesome beauty, I concluded. These were the beginnings of my learning to praise God. Perhaps that was also how David, the psalmist, learned, as he kept his father's sheep through the watches of the night. It sounds as though it might have been. 'The heavens declare the glory of God; the skies proclaim the work of his hands' (Psalm 19:1). Sometimes I even prayed, after a fashion. They were selfish prayers for sure, as I thought God was there to answer yes to all my wishes and whims. I still marvel at his infinite patience and incredible long-suffering!

Living in Australia was equally interesting. My poor English didn't encourage prospective employers to take me on. But eventually a launch hostess job came up, and then I worked as a waitress on the Barrier Reef of Queensland. It was great and I learned a lot of English. But I became restless once again. Was this all that life was about? I was searching but didn't know what for.

I moved on to Tasmania, staying there with a lovely young couple who were Christians. We had met several months earlier on a camping trip. Unfortunately I don't remember if, or what of, their witness touched me. I do remember that in those days the French Bible I had won at a competition in Belgium some years previously was in fairly frequent use. The snag was that I read it as some would a horoscope, looking to see if today or the near future would work out all right for me. I don't remember any verse that spoke directly to my heart. But what I'll never forget is the day, when walking in the street, I was suddenly deeply convicted of sin. How I

105

knew I wasn't right with God! There was no vision, like Paul's on the Damascus road, nor any voices: I just felt profoundly awful.

## Unspeakable peace

Since in those days churches still kept their doors unlocked, they offered an opportunity to slip into the perfect silence of their walls. I knelt at the back of one, earnestly praying for the first time ever, that God would forgive me for all the ways in which I had offended him. I knew that God heard me, because the unspeakable peace that followed was as overwhelming as the sense of wretchedness that preceded it. Such peace that I had not known before marked the turning point in my life, one which I have never since regretted.

My Roman Catholic background encouraged me to think that, if I now did good works, God would find me more acceptable. I had a mental picture of nuns working in darkest Africa, they seemed to me to be the model in that line. Not that I ever aspired to be a nun, far from it, but how would a travel agent cum boat hostess cum waitress be of any use in such places? So, against all my natural inclinations, I considered training as a nurse. That, till then, happened to be the very last option in my list of professional priorities. To my great surprise I was accepted for nurses' training and I learned to enjoy it.

## Incognito – in jeans?

I lived in the nurses' home and passed in front of the Reformed Church building every day on my way to classes or work. At weekends all my friends went home and I often stayed alone. One day, out of boredom really, I decided to pop into that church, as incognito as possible, and briefly too. Little did I know that this medium sized congregation knew each other like the palms of their hands, and my going there, in jeans (!) was as noticeable as putting a huge bandage on a sore thumb. The irony was that I arrived far too early and found myself at the end of a back pew, against the wall, having to wait at the end of the service for the church to empty from the front pews first. Who says that the Lord does not have a sense of humour?

The members of that congregation had read their Bibles. 'Keep on loving each other as brothers. Do not forget to entertain strangers' (Heb. 13:1-2). I was awed by the fact that people who didn't know me at all should invite me into their homes for lunch that very first day. However, I didn't understand a word of that first sermon, or the second or the third. But, as I continued to go and listened to the gospel being preached, the penny finally dropped. Of course the good works I hoped to do would not earn me acceptance with God. Only what Jesus did on the cross could do that. Did I, could I, should I not accept him who gave himself for me so that I might have life and have it abundantly? Suddenly it made perfect sense and how grateful I was to accept him as my Saviour!

## From Scotland to Somalia

Was I free from this desire to serve God in places like darkest Africa? I asked myself. Well, I reasoned, I no longer had to do something like that to earn salvation, but might I not do it to thank him for what he had done for me? Of course I could, which is why my life became what it is now. After studying midwifery in Scotland and tropical diseases in London, I worked for six months in a refugee camp in Somalia, then six months in India. By the end of that time I realised how little I knew of God's Word and how vital it was to acquire a better grounding in it.

## ...and Peru

Glasgow became the centre of attraction for the following fifteen months which I spent at its famous Bible Training College. I then served for three years in the Northern Andes of Peru under the umbrella of the Free Church of Scotland; while with Tear Fund, four years were spent in the Central African Republic and three years in a jungle area of Peru. Recent further studies have helped me put in better perspective all the notions of Primary Health Care I have been involved in overseas, encouraging me even more to share skills with those who have little access to education, yet have tremendous gifts to reach out to their own people.

I really have nothing to be proud of except God. Had it not been for him, where would I be today? I marvel that, even in my non-believing days, he kept me from what could have been a very different life indeed. What I have learnt is that God respects our personalities and uses the gifts he has given us to glorify him wherever we are ... if we let him do so. He also uses our past experiences to help us meet our needs of today. It isn't for nothing that I learned to climb trees as a child, when on many occasions rivers have had to be crossed on tree logs and branches, both in Peru and Africa; or that I learned to drive a motorbike for fun on a tourist resort years ago and found that to be an asset for my work since then. I can't help but say that God is so wonderful!

## My Father's tender care

John writes at the end of his Gospel, 'Jesus did many other things as well. If every one of them were written down, I suppose that even the whole world would not have room for the books that would be written' (21:25). That is so true! Even if I had to write accounts of God's faithfulness to me, there would be many shelves of books. Just one or two examples may warm the reader's heart.

They do mine, as I remember his faithful and providential care of me.

One of them takes me back to Peru. Seven of us were driving in a brand new vehicle in the Andes, going to an important church gathering across the mountain range. At one stage, for no apparent reason, the driver seemed to lose control of the car. He swerved (power steering can have disadvantages at times!) to avoid the mountain wall, therefore headed straight for the abyss, accelerating instead of braking and plunging us pretty fast into nothingness. Have you ever wondered what it must be like to be a piece of clothing in a tumble dryer? I think I know – pretty sore and even messy! The car turned three times on itself in mid-air before landing on its side on top of some trees that were holding on for their lives to the cliff side. What is extraordinary is that the day before this accident occurred, the owner of that piece of land would have cut his trees down had it not been so hot. His not doing so prevented us diving another 1,000 metres below to a certain death. Imagine how we felt as we crawled, bruised but safe, out of the window of that car on the tree tops! How much praise we expressed to the One who protected us so miraculously.

Another vivid recollection of God's faithfulness takes me back to Nepal. Two of us were visiting a missionary friend in Kathmandu.

It was night and time to sleep, when all of a sudden an oppressive darkness tried to overwhelm me. What happened is so hard to describe in words but it was obvious that the darkness wasn't merely the obscurity of the night. And it wasn't an external darkness, it was within me and it was evil. It was so obviously evil that it took me immediately to my knees, trembling and pleading with Jesus not to leave me. I couldn't think of any elaborate words, except to repeat Jesus' name. In floods of tears I pled with him not to leave me, never leave me. How long this lasted is hard to say but, when it did, I went back to bed, still shaken, to find that in no time the same thing repeated itself. I clung to my Bible, in a very different way than I had done before I became a Christian, desperate to find a word of promise that indeed God would not leave me. The struggle was intense and I felt desperately weak. So much so that in the wee hours of the morning, still crying and too scared to sleep, I went to my two friends for prayerful help because this 'thing' waved its way in and out like the tide of a mighty ocean. We prayed for a long while.

It was God's word that brought me the peace that only he can give. He proved, yet again, his love, his kindness and his faithfulness, through these verses: 'Let us hold unswervingly to the hope we profess, for he who promised is faithful' (Hebrews 10:23), and 'Do not throw away your confidence; it will be richly rewarded. You need to persevere so that when you have done the will of God, you will receive what he has promised. For in just a very little while, "He who is coming will come and will not delay. But my righteous one will live by faith. And if he shrinks back, I will not be pleased with him." But we are not of those who shrink back and are destroyed, but of those who believe and are saved' (Hebrews 10:35-39).

**Every day is a miracle**
I don't think everyone needs to go through an abyss, physical or spiritual, to prove God's faithfulness, or even to try it as each day brings signs of it in big and small ways. Every day is a miracle, showing how dependent we are or at least ought to be on God. I discovered that when two boats I was on ran on to rocks (one made it safely, the other started to sink, fortunately near land!), twice trains on which I was a passenger were derailed – nothing too dramatic but we were far away from any help and both times at very high and freezing altitudes; and on one occasion, when for what appeared to be ages I was completely lost in thick mist while walking on my own on top of Table Mountain in Cape Town.

God's faithfulness and his perfect timing and intimate knowledge of my needs have also been evident in my former and more recent student days. The providential provision of funds that helped finance the courses, spoke of his care, as did cheques arriving in the post, money kindly slipped in my pocket or gifts in kind, even a smile or a hug when the sailing was tough, exactly at the time when supplies were at their lowest. How God used people who were receptive to his prompting to supply my every need. It has been a lesson to me never to postpone or brush off any inner urge or prompting to act, inadequate though my actions may seem, knowing that God can use them to his honour and glory.

Life has been so interesting and challenging. Unlike Paul I was never flogged nor lowered down a wall in a basket, nor have I met an impressive list of troubles such as his: bandits, prison, hunger, nakedness, beaten with rods, exposed to death (2 Cor 11:23-29). And I thank God for that. But I can and do identify with Paul's conclusion, 'When I am weak, then I am strong' (2 Cor 12:10). And, like the apostle, I have found God's promise to be true, 'My grace is sufficient for you, for my power is made perfect in weakness' (2 Cor 12:9).

This is an account of God's dealings with me. He has moulded me and shaped me to do what he has wanted me to do. And he has much more work to do on me before he takes me home to heaven. But one thing I must do now, and I must do it always for as long as I live, and that is that

I must trust him, sometimes with the hardest of trials. That is my duty. It is also my joy, for I have found him to be utterly trustworthy.

# OLIVER McALLISTER

My childhood home was a happy one. Like many Irish Catholic families, ours was large. There were nine of us: Dad, Mum, my six sisters and myself. We were close to each other, and caring. But in 1970 into that happy home came a tragedy that was to change everything, for nothing would ever be the same again. I was eleven years old. My father, a plumbing and heating engineer, needed wakened in the afternoon to go out on his shift. I ran up the stairs. His door was slightly open. Seeing his leg hanging over the edge of the bed I decided to give him a fright. 'Come on, Daddy!' I shouted, grabbing his leg. 'Its time you got up for work.' But his leg was heavy and cold. I knew right away what had happened. It was the day before Christmas, and my dad had died in his sleep.

We were strict Roman Catholics. All around our house were holy pictures and little crucifixes. It was to a picture of the Sacred Heart of Jesus, which hung above my bed, that I ran for help.

With a broken heart I cried to the picture on the wall, sobbing the prayer that my daddy would come back to life again. I believed that when I would go back into his room and grab him by the leg, everything would be all right. He would jump up shouting, 'What are you at?' But that was not to be.

Before I went downstairs to tell my sisters, I paused and looked into my dad's face. I had known from a very early age that inside each one of us is a soul that leaves our bodies when we die. As I stared at his body, I knew with a certainty that my dad's soul had left his body. Where is he now? I wondered. Where is he now?

## Big questions for a little boy

Dad had been a good man: drink and bad language were not used in our home. His family was everything to him, and he associated with few outside of it. Has he gone to heaven? I asked myself. Is my dad away to be with God? But then an awful thought struck me. What if he wasn't good enough to go to heaven? Where is he then? Could he have gone to hell? I thought about hell and the kind of people who went there: murderers and people like that. No, I reasoned, no way would my dad go to hell. My dad was too good for hell.

So where had he gone? All our religious teaching told us the answer to that. Dad had gone to purgatory. We believed it was up to us to get him out of purgatory and into heaven. And, because we loved him so much, we did all that we could. We said prayers for my dad. We had masses said for the good of his soul. And we put money into the chapel for his release. There was no way we wanted our dad to spend years and years in purgatory when our prayers and masses and money could get him out of there. Every now and then mum would give us an envelope to take to the priest, asking him to offer up the next mass for our dad. I took some money of my own when I went. Going into the chapel, I would walk to the front beside the altar. Putting my money in the box, I would light a candle and pray to the statue of the Virgin Mary, fervent prayers that she would ask her Son to release my dad from purgatory.

A thought ate at my young heart. Where would I go if I died? Without a shadow of doubt I knew I wasn't good enough to go to heaven. But, on the other hand, with all the good works I had done even as a little boy, I felt I wasn't bad enough to go to hell. I lived with the knowledge that if I were to die I would go, like my dad, to purgatory. And there I would depend on my family's prayers, their money and their masses for my soul, if I were ever to be released. It was a frightening thought.

**Where would I go?**
Although that troubled me off and on, most of the time I put it to the back of my mind and got on with my life. There were, however, occasions when the thought confronted me violently. If I saw a hearse passing, it brought me up short, and I found myself wondering if the person whose remains it was carrying had gone to heaven or hell or purgatory. And always that question – where would I go if I died? On one occasion, when I saw a boy knocked down and killed, I was tortured with questions. Where was his soul? Fear had a big grip on my life.

As a teenager I became an altar boy in the chapel, helping the priest with the mass. I thought if I helped him, went to mass and did good works, God would see the life I was leading and be pleased enough with me that he would take me to heaven. After all, I had been baptised as a baby, took my first communion when I was eight, and was confirmed a year or two after that. Surely, I decided, they were my tickets to heaven. But there was always a niggling doubt. I did my best, at least most of the time, but was my best good enough?

**The Lord's business**
After leaving school in 1975 I went to work for a Christian man who was not afraid to speak about his faith or his Saviour. He was a businessman,

and put up with no shirkers. I remember one day he said he'd stand over me till I finished a job of work. And he did. As I worked, from 11am until 4pm, he talked to me about the things of God. His business was important to him, but when the Lord's business needed to be done, that took priority. He told me I was a sinner who had come short of the glory of God. I had never heard language like that before. Only bad people were sinners, after all. I didn't think I knew anyone who was really bad enough to be called a sinner. Good people who did wrong things were not sinners in my young mind. He told me how the Lord Jesus went to Calvary, there to die for sinners. My boss testified to his own faith and God's faithfulness. 'Oliver,' he concluded, 'I realised through someone witnessing to me, that I was a sinner before God and that the Lord Jesus stood, with outstretched arms, waiting to forgive me for all my filthy dirty sins and receive me. I cried out from the depths of my heart and told him I was a sinner and that I wanted to be saved.'

This was all new to me. As much as I had gone to mass, to missions, to novenas, I had never heard the like. It seemed so right, that I was almost persuaded. But, when I walked away from work that afternoon, it was as if the devil opened up my heart, lifted out the seed that had been sown, and threw it away.

But life went on. And the years that followed

brought changes and challenges. In 1978 I met Deirdre and we were married the following year. When, in 1986, our last daughter Leanne was born joining her sisters, Fiona and Lorraine, our family was complete.

It was later, from the late 1980s onwards, when I was working as a bus driver, that God was to speak to me again. He gave me such a concern for my soul that I went with my daughter, Lorraine, to a shrine at Mountmellick, in the south of Ireland. Thousands of people went there to see a statue of the Virgin Mary moving and to hear the statue speaking. Someone told me that they had seen the face of the Lord Jesus Christ there. It was with yearning of soul that I went. Lorraine and I stood at the statue on a winter's night in the pouring rain, praying the rosary from the depths of our hearts. I prayed and prayed but nothing happened. I went with one purpose in mind, to see the face of Jesus, but I left disappointed and disillusioned, with my tears mingling with the rain on my face.

**Hungry but unsatisfied**
I used to watch people going to church on Sundays with their Bibles and wondered why I didn't have one, and why people going to the mass didn't need Bibles. Something in me yearned for God's Word. I tried to find it in my missal, a little book with a mass for every day of the year.

But it left me frustrated. There was nothing in it to satisfy my needs.

Once again, I was confronted with the question that plagued me. A poor man who got on to my bus collapsed and died. Nothing could be done to save him. Having run to call an ambulance I came back and knelt down beside his body. Putting my mouth to his ear, I whispered, 'O my God, I'm very sorry for having sinned against thee because thou art good. With the help of grace I'll never sin again.' I prayed that God would hear that prayer as if it came from the dead man's lips. Where was his soul? I asked myself, after the ambulance men had taken his body away. Had God heard that prayer? And the old question came back again to haunt me. Where would I go if I died?

That very afternoon a toddler in a buggy on my bus choked on a sweet. Hearing her mum's screams I looked in the mirror and saw the child's purple face and terrified eyes. I dashed to the back of the bus, upturned the buggy, and slapped the wee thing on the back to dislodge the sweet. I was never so glad to hear a child cry in all my life. But that day left me deeply shaken. What was happening to me? I had come face to face with eternity twice in one day. And the question came back yet again. Where would I go if I died?

**Questions and answers**

Two or three months after that I was with Trevor Holmes, a fellow bus driver. He had lost his son in an accident some time before.

'Trevor, tell me this,' I asked him, 'how did you ever get over the death of your boy?'

'The Lord helped me,' he replied.

And I knew from the way he said it that here was a man who knew God. I had religion, but Trevor had a relationship. I depended on rituals while he depended on the Lord Jesus Christ. That night, and every night for the following week, I travelled home on Trevor's bus. And we talked.

'Oliver, have you got a Bible?' he asked one evening after I had contradicted some things he said.

I felt embarrassed and ashamed. 'Sure I've got a Bible,' I lied.

When I got off his bus that night, it was as though the Holy Spirit spoke right to me, telling me to get myself a Bible. As soon as I could the next day I went to a shop that sold holy things. There were pictures of all the saints I had prayed to and statues of the Virgin Mary. Hanging on the walls were crucifixes on which was the figure of our Lord, with a trickle of blood painted on his hands, feet and side. I took £10 from my pocket.

'Can I have a Bible, please?' I asked the woman in the shop.

'I'm sorry,' she replied. 'We don't sell them.'

You could have knocked me down with a feather. She gave me directions to a shop that would have one, and when I got there it was almost as if the Bible was reaching off the shelf to meet me.

## My very own Bible

I went from the shop to pick up my bus and start my shift. Before my first run I sat in the driver's seat reading my Bible, my very own Bible. I remember my thoughts. I'll read it as fast as I can. I'll get as much out of it as I'm able to. Now I'm going to find out the truth. Sitting there on the bus I read the first five chapters of Genesis. Then I came to verse 3 of chapter 6. 'My Spirit shall not always strive with man' (AV). The Holy Spirit used that to make me stop and think.

It was only then that I realised that my bus was half full. People had given me money and I'd given them all sorts of tickets. I don't know how much change I gave them or if they got any at all. They must have wondered about me, thinking that I was so deep in the Bible that I could neither see nor hear what was going on round about me. God was speaking to me, telling me to watch myself, reminding me that he wasn't playing a game, and that I shouldn't play a game with my soul either, for I might lose. Putting the bus into gear I raced through my route to give me time at the other end to read some more. If the police had caught me that day I think I would have lost my licence.

I wasn't very long into my reading when I started to get lost. I couldn't wait to get on to Trevor's bus that night.

'I've an apology to make to you,' I told him. 'Remember you asked me if I had a Bible and I said I had? Well I hadn't. But I was ashamed to admit it, and I didn't want you to be one up on me. When I got off your bus it was as though God told me to go and get one.'

Trevor's eyes filled up and I thought he was going to cry. 'That's amazing,' he said. 'Last night when I went home I told Myrtle about our conversation. Then I got down on my knees and prayed that God would show me what to say to you.'

I told him what I'd been reading, and he pointed me to other verses about calling on God when he is near. My heart was moved.

## God's Word speaks

The devil had dragged me down over the previous months, and I let him do it. I smoked, drank nearly every night and had lost a fortune on bets. So bad did my drinking become that my wife, Deirdre, sat in the car waiting for me to get off the bus, just to stop me going to the pub. That night, when I got off Trevor's bus with my Bible, she looked at me hard.

'That's a Bible,' she said.

I told her I had bought it. And I remember her reaction well.

'Oliver, listen till I tell you something. You know what they say about people who read Bibles? They crack up. You're going to crack up, as if you're not bad enough the way you are just now.'

Things did change. The desire to go to the pub left me. I wanted to stay at home reading my Bible to find out the truth. Eventually I came to the part in John's Gospel where Nicodemus, a man much more religious than I ever was, asked the Lord Jesus just what I wanted to know. I read Jesus' answer, that we need to be born again. I didn't know what he meant, but the Lord went on to explain it. That I had been born of the flesh I knew fine well, and I knew too that I had not been born of the Spirit.

I read on. In John 6:37 I found Jesus' words, 'Whoever comes to me I will never drive away.' And again in John 14:6 he said, 'I am the way and the truth and the life. No-one comes to the Father except through me.' What about all the prayers I've prayed to the saints? I asked myself. And I concluded that either I was right and this Bible was wrong, or I was wrong and this Bible was right. And I meant to find out which.

**The Great High Priest**

Then one night in 1989, as I read of the Lord's crucifixion while Deirdre watched the television, tears started to run down my face. I went upstairs and thought of his agony. Guilt overwhelmed me and I cried out to God for mercy. And right there and then the Lord saved me. That day, 23rd October 1989, I went to confession to the priest, the Great High Priest, the Lord Jesus. I cried sore and I prayed hard. I knew what Deirdre's reaction would be – and I was right. When I told her I was saved she looked at me as though I had two heads. 'Didn't I tell you if you started reading that Bible you'd crack up?' she demanded.

The devil gave us a hard time for the next year and a half. He did everything in his power to prevent household salvation. Then one day Deirdre came to me when I arrived home from work with the Bible in her hand. 'What does this mean?' she asked. 'And what does that mean?' I told her that it was God's word and that I believed it. That very day my wife had a desire to go to a meeting at church, and while she was there she came to the Lord. It was not easy for her as her mother had threatened to disown her if that ever happened. But God overruled that situation. Instead of disowning her, she accepted that Deirdre had made up her mind and that it couldn't be changed.

**To God be the glory!**

We have three daughters, Fiona, Lorraine and Leanne. Leanne came to me one night when I was getting ready to go to a prayer meeting. 'Daddy,' she said, 'I want to be saved and to have my sins forgiven. I want to go to heaven when I die.' We knelt down on our knees and she asked the Lord to come into her life and cleanse her from her sin. And then came the best of all birthday presents. Lorraine was converted on my birthday, on our way home from a meeting we had attended together. What the devil had fought against the Lord did.

My testimony does not end with my conversion and the conversion of the ones I love most in this world. It is an ongoing thing. I can testify to God's goodness day by day and hour by hour. May all the glory and the praise be his.

# LINDSAY BENN

It is said that life begins at forty. Well, my fortieth birthday passed not so long ago, and that certainly was a busy and interesting year for me, especially as my husband, Wallace, was consecrated as a bishop in the Church of England. But my new life began a long time before that.

The Bible teaches that God Almighty, the creator of heaven and earth, is our heavenly Father. He knows and cares for us long before we are consciously aware of him. Psalm 139 is one of my favourites. It speaks of God's intimate knowledge and loving care of us before ever we were born. 'For you created my inmost being; you knit me together in my mother's womb' (Psalm 139:13). God even knew those who follow him before the beginning of time. He 'chose us in him (Christ) before the creation of the world to be holy and blameless in his sight' (Ephesians 1:4). That's mind-boggling!

**Life in a God-fearing home**
I was the first of three children born to my parents,
Alan and Dorothy Develing. Brought up in a God-
fearing home, I was taken (not sent) to Sunday
school where my Mum was a teacher. I am so
grateful to God for the hard work and dedication
of those Sunday School teachers who faithfully
taught me, reinforcing my Christian upbringing,
in church halls that had ceilings that seemed to
reach the sky! It was completely natural for me
to read the Bible and pray. But, although I knew
quite a bit about God at that stage, I did not know
him personally.

At the age of eleven or twelve I moved into
the Girl Covenanters, a girls' Bible class that met
on Sundays, and on a week night for general fun
and hilarity. The Covenanters were to be another
part of God's plan to find me and bring me to a
relationship with him. He also used the
confirmation class I attended when I was
fourteen. Covenanters organised regional and
national events which, after a day of sports
competitions, Bible recitations and Bible quizzes,
ended with us gathering together for a time of
singing, prayer and a talk. I remember little of
the talk I heard at the Rally that year, but it was
as if God addressed me personally. I even
wondered if anyone else had noticed!

**Does Jesus go with you everywhere?**

The speaker concluded his talk with the question, 'Does Jesus go with you everywhere that you go?' I remember he explained that we must neither go to, nor be found in, places that we would not like Jesus to find us if he came back. While that was not my particular problem God showed me that I was not allowing my belief in him to permeate every area of my life. Young as I was, I was beginning to keep God in pockets of religious activity. The thought of Jesus being in school with me, or of my talking to my friends about him, had not really entered my consciousness. That night God challenged me to become a full time Christian. I asked him for forgiveness for all the wrong things I had done. He came into my life, filling me with his Holy Spirit. I was born again – that makes me about thirty years old now! So began my new life 'in Christ'. God had found me. He had accomplished in me what he had planned since the foundation of the world. But that was just the beginning.

My life didn't change dramatically when I became a Christian, but it did change for the better as I was constantly aware of God's presence with me. I could talk to him any time and anywhere. And he spoke to me through his Word. I remember being very struck by the verse, 'Cast all your cares on him for he cares for you' (1 Peter 5:7), in the middle of an English lesson because it was written on the side of my pencil!

At school I was conscious both that I needed to share my faith with my friends, and that they would be watching to see if my life and actions matched. One of my teachers often teased me about being a Christian. But the same man unwittingly gave me many opportunities to share my faith in classroom assemblies, mainly because he didn't like doing them himself! There were believing teachers too, who were a great encouragement. I helped to lead the Junior Christian Union in the school, which proved to be a wonderful opportunity. It allowed me to encourage young Christians in their faith, and to develop my own understanding of how relevant the Bible is to every age.

## Seeking the curate's advice

After being a Christian for a couple of years I began to wonder if God was prodding me in the direction of full time Christian work. I had a growing interest in the South American Missionary Society and the work of missionaries in general. As some others at church also suggested the possibility of full time Christian work, I went to see the curate, Wallace Benn, for advice. Wallace, who is now my husband, often relates that story with great amusement. Unknown to me he had fallen in love with me and was prayerfully and patiently waiting until I was eighteen to ask me to go out with him! How he managed to conceal his feelings for so long still amazes me. On that occasion he gave me careful and unbiased advice.

Since the age of six I had wanted to be a primary school teacher and was working in that direction, although I still had two years of secondary school, three years at university and one year postgraduate training still to do! He suggested that I continued to pray, asking God to show me what he wanted me to do, all the while working hard to gain the necessary qualifications. After all, he concluded, I would be more helpful in South America as a teacher than as an enthusiastic sixteen year old! His advice made a great deal of sense and I continued at senior school, then took up a place at Sheffield University where I read Biblical Studies.

Falling in love, studying and travelling were to be the main activities of the next three years. Wallace and I began to 'go out' with each other shortly after my eighteenth birthday. We had a wonderful summer before I went away to university. Although the course was excellent, it was difficult to be so far apart. Engaged during my first year, we were married the week after I graduated! God had been preparing me for a long time for the job of minister's wife. This was part of his plan for me. He had created in me a desire to serve him full time. Romans 15:5-6 was the biblical advice on which we embarked on married life. 'May the God who gives endurance and encouragement give you a spirit of unity among yourselves as you follow Christ Jesus, so that with one heart and mouth you may glorify the God and Father of our Lord Jesus Christ.'

## More about the curate

While I was at University, Wallace became the curate at St. Mary's Church in Cheadle, Cheshire. And it was there that we spent the first three happy years of our married life. I spent the initial year juggling teacher training, housework and church activities. We thought that there might be a need for that professional training some time in the future. But it was an exhausting year and I was relieved to qualify and apply myself full time to being a minister's wife.

Our main responsibility in Cheadle was the running of a large church-based youth work. The group of teenagers who met weekly for Bible studies soon filled, then outgrew, our home. We well remember one occasion when a salesman called trying to sell football pools. From the doorway he could see teenagers everywhere. They were all through the hall, up the stairs and on the landing. Wallace was in the middle of them, Bible in hand. It took a good five minutes of laughter after the door shut behind the poor man before anyone was fit to continue the study.

We also met with the young people on Saturday evenings for games and a talk given by a speaker. Sundays were busy with services. And an after-church meeting was led by the young people themselves. These were exciting days, richly blessed by the fact that we had the privilege of seeing many of them entering into a personal relationship with Jesus.

We held missions in all the local secondary schools, taking lessons and organising concerts with Christian rock bands who were skilled in explaining the gospel message to young people. One particular evening sticks in my mind because I was scared stiff. About 1,000 teenagers crowded into a school hall and trouble was brewing in one corner of it. God showed us he was very much in control that night, even though we didn't feel that we were! The amplification system blew and stopped the concert. The troublemakers left, a repair was effected and the concert resumed. We were able to talk to those who were really interested and they were able to hear.

It was hard to leave Cheadle when the time came to do so. The youth group had grown to just over 200, making it one of the largest church youth groups in the country. But, although we loved them dearly, the Lord had work for us to do elsewhere. Wallace had done two assistant jobs and it was now time for him to become a vicar and in charge of his own parish. And that was the parish of Audley in north Staffordshire. The ancient village of Audley, which is mentioned in the Doomsday Book, had been surrounded by suburban housing with farm land on the outskirts. And, as far as we could tell, Wallace was only the second Evangelical minister in seven hundred years!

## Joys and sorrows

We were overjoyed at the birth of our daughter Jessica in 1983, particularly as we had suffered a miscarriage before that. As she was a 'local' in the eyes of the villagers, such was their admiration of her that going to buy a loaf of bread could take an hour. Imagine our devastation when, at the age of eighteen months, our dear little daughter pulled a tray of tea off the work top in the kitchen, badly scalding her face, chest and arm. The hospital doctor warned us that she would need a facial skin graft. We prayed and prayed. Our whole church family prayed with us and for us. Someone sent me flowers at that time with a card of the well-known poem 'Footprints'. How true its words are. God carried us through deep dark days until he could put our feet down safely on the other side. Reading the psalms was a great help. 'I will take refuge in the shadow of your wings until the disaster has passed' (Psalm 57:1), spoke words of comfort to us on the day of Jessica's accident.

When we returned to the hospital with our little daughter two weeks later, the doctor said, 'It is a miracle. Her skin has healed much better than it should.' We were able to testify to him that our God is capable of miracles and that ultimately all healing is in his hands. How thankful we were and are to our heavenly Father. Jessica has one tiny mark on her collar bone that she calls her miracle mark! It reminds us all how the Lord saved her face.

Four years later there was again great celebration in the Benn household when James, our son, was born. By then we knew that we were on the move again. With five week old James, and his four year old sister Jessica, we moved to St. Peter's Church in Harold Wood, Essex. This seemed a big thing for us as we had always hoped never to go to London! But God had made it very clear through reading Scripture together, and the advice of wise and trusted friends, that this was the way ahead. We were embarking on a further stage of God's plan for our lives, assured that he knew what he was doing.

St. Peter's is a large evangelical Anglican church seventeen miles north east of London. Although many people commute to work, there is still a village identity to Harold Wood. The people were welcoming and friendly and we settled in quickly. It has been our experience that, however different our surroundings might be, people's need of Jesus as their Saviour and friend is always the same. Wallace and the staff team set about preaching and equipping the congregation for the Christian life. It was thrilling to see people coming to faith, and to witness their enthusiasm and eagerness to bring their friends to hear the good news of Jesus for themselves.

The time in Harold Wood seemed to zoom past. When both children were at school I began teaching, part time, children with learning difficulties who attended our local primary school. It was interesting to see how God used the training with which he had equipped me. Wallace became chairman of the school's governing body, and the headmistress was kind and gracious enough to give us, as a church, many opportunities to be involved in the school and to talk to the children about Jesus.

## A bolt out of the blue

It was when our lives seemed busier than ever that Wallace became suddenly unwell with a very high fever. Little were we to know that this was to be the beginning, both of a long illness, and of a year that would see dramatic changes in our lives. The following day, and by then we had decided he had a bad dose of flu, a letter came asking him to meet the Bishop of Chichester to discuss the possibility of him becoming the next Bishop of Lewes on the south coast of England.

Now that was a bolt out of the blue! Completely stunned, we prayed frantically for guidance. It was not something we had ever imagined would happen. To say it was a real shock is no exaggeration.

But events overtook us in 1996. Wallace was admitted to hospital with suspected pneumonia. This was a dreadful time. I watched anxiously as his health deteriorated and no adequate diagnosis was made. Gradually walking became difficult for him, and any effort left him completely exhausted. Eventually, after referral to the infectious diseases department, it was found that a streptococcal infection had triggered a severe immune reaction. We clung to each other and to our sovereign God. Although Wallace was weak and I was weary, we tried to read two psalms each day. God used them to encourage us constantly, even when we were at our lowest. 'My soul finds rest in God alone; my salvation comes from him. He alone is my rock and my salvation; he is my fortress, I shall never be shaken' (Psalm 62:1-2).

For four months Wallace was able to do very little, and there was no question of his taking part in any public ministry. We prayed, wondering if we had any ministry left at all, never mind the possibility of becoming a bishop. Feeling that we were in a long tunnel with light at the other end, we struggled on, but seemed to move no nearer the light. We trusted that God would lead us. And it seemed to us, as we pondered on it and prayed it through, that if Wallace's health returned he should do the job of bishop.

The Bishop of Chichester was endlessly patient, believing that Wallace was God's man for the job. Because we were sworn to secrecy we couldn't discuss our dilemma with anyone. We struggled on, knowing that God is sovereignly in control of all the events of our lives and that nothing, even ill health, can get in the way of his plans. The Lord always has a purpose in suffering, and, although there were many things that we did not understand, we were brought to realise again that what God wants more than anything else is our loving relationship with him. He rescues us and saves us and longs for us to walk close to him as his adopted and dependant children.

Slowly we edged toward the light at the end of that tunnel. My husband began to preach again and by Christmas he coped with all the services, though he was completely exhausted in between them. In the new year we saw a top London consultant who assured us that Wallace was on the road to a complete recovery but that it would take another few months. What a relief! And how thankful we were to God.

# The Bishop of Lewes

The next few months passed in a whirl of frantic activity. Consecration day was set for the 1st of May 1997 and there were endless things to be done. The last night of April was spent in Lambeth Palace at the invitation of the Archbishop of Canterbury and Mrs. Carey. As we listened to the chimes of Big Ben every fifteen minutes through the early hours of the morning, we reflected on the events leading up to this special day. 'What are we doing here?' we wondered. But we knew the answer. Our great and sovereign God had brought us through what seemed like a wilderness to change and remould us, so fitting us for the new job he had for us to do. And, as we faced the enormity of it, we knew our Father did not expect us to do it in our strength but in his strength, and with his constant love and support.

So began another unknown: a new area, a new job, a new house, new schools for the children and a church to find and belong to. Weak and trembling though we are, we have found him true to all his promises. Wallace has been Bishop of Lewes since 1997, and our Father God has been by our side every step along the way, even when we have not been aware of him. 'My salvation and my honour depend on God; He is my mighty rock, my refuge. Trust in him at all times, O people; pour out your hearts to him, for God is our refuge' (Psalm 62:7-8).

# TIM TRUMPER

In the final analysis, nobody enters life in a right relationship to God, not even a Welshman of Presbyterian stock! For all the spiritual privileges inherited at birth, I began life out of step with my Maker (Psalm 51: 5). Although not intended as ends in themselves, these privileges did set me apart from much of the rest of humanity even in rural Wales. Especially important was the availability of a church where the Holy Scriptures were revered as God's Word, and my parents who consistently took me to hear it being taught and applied. At church I heard the gospel powerfully and urgently calling me to be right with God by looking to Christ who has made it possible.

**Born a Pembrokeshire boy**
My life began in 1966 in Pembrokeshire, in the south west corner of Wales. I was the third of four children born to Peter and Margaret Trumper. My father was an unlikely Presbyterian minister. Educated in an English public school, during the war his parents moved to Cardiff, where he became a Dean Scholar in the choir at

Llandaff Cathedral. Later still he opted for a staunch Atheism during his time at Cardiff Castle of Music and Drama until his sudden conversion to Christ. Despite this, he continued into stage and screen acting until God called him into the Christian ministry a few years later. My mother, on the other hand, was a nurse and midwife by training, whose father – a Cardiff electrician – had tried to 'beat Christianity out of her' during her teenage years. Eventually he too became a Christian in his late forties and latterly served as a founder-elder of the church in which Dad ministered in Clarbeston Road, near Haverfordwest in Pembrokeshire.

Being a minister's son can be somewhat embarrassing and inconvenient at times! As Dad used to put it, the children of Christian homes often suffer for the faith of their parents. Consequently, he and Mum sought to provide us with as normal an upbringing as possible. Outside of school, Saturday mornings were often spent walking Lucy our Pembrokeshire Corgi along the beautiful beaches of the county. On wet Saturdays we would go swimming at the local pool. As the years unfolded Andy, Ceri, Karl and I variously chose to join the Cubs, Brownies, Scouts, and Army Cadets. In addition, Karl and I spent many a Saturday playing football and cricket for Narberth at under 13 and under 15 levels. In fact, we were fully integrated into the community.

## Raised a 'preacher's kid'

Two things did stand out about our upbringing. First, we would read a passage from the Bible and pray as a family each morning and evening. In the evenings this took longer because Dad would run a competition throughout each school term. Two points were given for every correct answer to a question on the Bible reading, one point for a half-correct answer and, of course, no points for the wrong answer. It was a fun way to learn about what the Bible has to say. Once prayers were over we would often test Dad's knowledge of the Scriptures by picking out a verse at random and challenging him to tell us where it came from. Regularly frustrated by how difficult it was to catch him out, we quickly observed how important he considered the Bible to be.

Then there were Sundays. Generally speaking, each Sunday morning and evening were spent listening to Dad preach. His evangelistic sermons were particularly memorable because they were of most relevance to me. Always graphic and passionate they were often based on the narrative portions of the gospels. The renowned preacher Dr. Martyn Lloyd-Jones, a native of the neighbouring county of Cardiganshire, once said of him, 'There's a man by the name of Trump... Trump... Trumpet... and by all accounts he's busy blowing it!' It is true. My father was a 'Trumpet' by calling and conviction. Indeed, never have I heard more powerful evangelistic preaching than that on which I was reared. The message he preached was ably accommodated to our young capacities in afternoon Sunday School. On alternate Sunday mornings we would miss the service in Clarbeston Road in order to support another Sunday School run by Harry Adams and Pat Davies in Llawhaden, a neighbouring village.

It would be dishonest to say that we never desired to be elsewhere. In fact, I often dreaded Mondays because my school pals would endlessly discuss all the 'telly' they had seen the day before. Missing 'telly', however, was not so much a problem to me but to them, for I dearly loved the people at church and they loved us too. Indeed, like others before me, I longed to be thirteen so that I could join the Young People's Fellowship (YPF) that met each Tuesday evening. These were happy times. The first half of YPF was spent chatting, weightlifting, playing football, table tennis and rounders, and the second half in Bible study or the discussion of some relevant topic. The leaders: Norman and Jacqui, John and Sîan, Rowland and Beat, Betty Stowell and John and Mair Murray – became real mainstays in the lives of the young people. Christianity seemed to flow *natural* from them. But it was not natural, that is the point!

## Outwardly decent, inwardly decadent

Although this sort of upbringing is commonly dismissed as 'brainwashing' these days, the things we were taught each week could only persuade us of the importance of being right with God. The teaching itself could not actually bring it about. Only God could do that by turning us to Jesus for salvation. Thus, my early life was characterised by an inevitable contradiction. Although I knew more about God than my peers at school and my elders in the neighbourhood, I did not know God personally. What follows then is the account of how God revealed himself to me.

Early on I learnt that humankind is alienated from God, and that although Christian parents and a healthy church-life can instil morality, they cannot bring us back into divine favour. Only Christ can accomplish that by reconciling us to God. Without reconciliation Christianity is reduced to the sort of familiar pew-filling that is characteristic of a respectable but hollow 'Churchianity'. Christianity by contrast focuses on God's gracious gift of his Son. It is not therefore a natural right.

Despite being outwardly upright I was always aware that there was something blocking me from my Maker. It was self-evident that if God is as holy as the Bible says he is then the presence of sin in my life, however apparently insignificant, must have separated me from him. None of the

145

spiritual privileges I possessed from birth could close this yawning gulf. They could merely highlight its existence and explain why the reality of Christ's presence was missing from my life. Although 'sin' is today a surprisingly alien concept given its prevalence in society, I knew that however sheltered I was from sin from without, nobody could protect me from the sin within. I was a sinner if for no other reason than that I had failed to love God as he deserves, with all my heart, soul and strength (Deuteronomy 6: 5). Self-love prevented me. Thus, instead of doing the will of God my Creator I was content to revel in sins of pride, lying, deceit, anger and hypocrisy. To begin with, however, I was unperturbed by the knowledge of my sin. I regarded my fallenness as a theological fact rather than as an affront to God. In Augustine's words, 'my pride-swollen face had closed up my eyes'.

This was convenient, for I firmly suspected that if God gave me his Son as my Saviour, then he would have me preaching him to others before too long! As much as I loved my father, I accepted that in society's increasingly secularised opinion he was a social oddball! Well, that was fine for him, so long as God did not call me to be the same. The best way to evade such a calling was to maintain the status quo. God would just have to remain content with my presence in church and no more.

# The long path to pardon

As early as the age of eight, however, my whole approach to God was brought into sharp focus when some young people from Cheltenham and Gloucester came to use the Sunday School hall for a summer holiday. It soon became obvious that one of the young people was intensely keen to evangelise our youth group. Although his zeal was most commendable, he would have realised with maturity that evangelism does not involve press-ganging. Eventually it became the turn of Karl and me to be conscripted. After reasoning with us for several hours, Lincoln took us to a secluded spot so that we could ask the Lord into our hearts. Too young to resist, we dutifully complied. As we did so the thought struck me that perhaps a belief in biblical doctrine was sufficient to save me after all. What else could faith possibly entail? Thus, it was no problem asking for forgiveness; we did that every day in family prayers. The crucial question, however, was whether there was a change of heart regarding the sin for which I requested forgiveness.

Confident of my true conversion, Lincoln kindly wrote to me on his return home in order to nurture me in the faith. Unfortunately, the letter was left in my trouser pocket as they went to the wash ... a basic error in any young boy's experience! When Mum found it, I told her that I had become a Christian even though I knew deep down that nothing had changed. God, however, providentially used my folly to keep before me the question of belief over the course of the next seven years. During that protracted period I bore the label 'Christian' uncomfortably in what was an impossible and an unpleasurable intensification of nominal Christianity.

My difficulty was that I just could not see what the Bible meant by 'believe'. If I believed all the biblical doctrines and was still out of touch with God, then how were all the famous gospel texts such as, 'For God so loved the world, that he gave his only begotten Son that whosoever believeth in him should not perish, but have everlasting life' (John 3:16, AV), to be understood. Too blind to see and too shy to ask, such supposedly crystal clear texts remained as clear as mud. That did not bother me until some unexpected deaths increased the urgency of resolving the matter.

**Chased on by death's shadow**

Two made a particular impression on me. First, there was Scott Kelly. Together we spent his last Saturday playing on The Moor in Narberth not knowing that we would never see each other again. Scott died of Meningitis early the next week. We were ten at the time. Conscious that detailed and inquisitive talk of death was a strong taboo and a giveaway of my private world, I cycled to the crematorium on the outskirts of the town. There I gazed at the bunch of wild primroses that had so recently been on Scott's coffin. Suddenly trusting in Christ really seemed to matter, for I might not have decades to work it out. So from then on I would often walk alone in the gardens of the crematorium, read the floral messages and watch the bereaved from a distance as they said farewell to their loved ones.

About the same time Paul Rees became a Christian. Mystified by my own standing before God, I could not wait to see him at church when news got around. Would he look different? Speak differently? Or act differently? Although he seemed much the same, when he later left for Scotland to become a ghillie his letters to the youth leaders gave evidence of genuine faith, the like of which was absent from my life. Thus, when he drowned in the River Dee near Aberdeen, I immediately began to wonder whether my relatives would have been so confident of my eternal destiny as Paul's were of his. Could it have been stated of me, as his uncle Norman had written next to Paul's name in the Sunday School register, that 'to be absent from the body is to be present with the Lord'? I doubted it.

**Off-loading Churchianity en route**
In attending school in Whitland, sixteen miles from church, there arose many possibilities for

living a double-life. Although still morally upright, there was no positive difference detectable between my friends and me. Daily I went without God's presence from my conscious experience simply because I had never crossed over from nominal to biblical Christianity. I could hide the fact from myself all the time, from the family much of the time, but eating away at me was the thought that I could not hide it at all from an all-seeing God who 'knows those who are his' (2 Timothy 2:19).

As it happened my parents were also cognisant of the situation. It became a relief that they were. After Church one Sunday morning my father, seeing my behavioural decline, took me to my bedroom. He quietly but sadly explained that he had always rejoiced in God that 25% of his children knew and loved the Lord; but he had to confess that he saw no evidence of the fact. With that he simply but piercingly asked, 'Do you love the Lord?' Now that is the question to ask any nominal Christian who hides behind a veneer of 'Churchianity', because it goes right to the heart of the matter. Had he asked anything else I could have dodged the issue. Instead the question proved to be a Heaven-sent opportunity to shrug off the facade. From that moment I determined to seek God, but even then I was conscious that in reality he was seeking me.

Over the following months my trite prayers

were swapped for an earnest prayer life. I began to confess to God that my fifteen year old life was indefensible in the light of his holiness. It became more obvious what the prophet Jeremiah meant when he declared that the human heart is beyond a cure (Jeremiah 17:9). I clearly understood what Jesus meant when he talked about the uncleanness that comes from the human heart (Mark 7:20-23). The fact that he was thinking of the Pharisees when he spoke of the heart's condition exposed my 'innocence' and undermined the sufficiency of my church attendance, for the Pharisees had spent even more time in 'church' than I did!

## Reconciled at last

Finally God was beginning to reveal something of what it means to believe. I had for long enough possessed the knowledge that informs faith. Now the Spirit of God was truly convicting me of my sin as he showed me its urgency. Intermingled with this faith was a sincere and a tearful repentance that increasingly saw the futility of comparing myself with others more blatantly sinful than myself. To God I was answerable because it was his standards that I had fallen short of. The fact that my sin was nothing by the world's standards was of no relevance to me. It was God's opinion that mattered for he alone knew me perfectly, inside and out. He alone could

151

terminate my natural estrangement from him, but not before bringing me to the feet of Jesus in my plea for salvation.

That summer I went for the first time to a Christian youth camp held in Colwyn Bay, North Wales, under the auspices of the Evangelical Movement of Wales (EMW). Although a year too young for the camp, I was providentially admitted to it. There I met many young people who evidently knew and loved the Lord and who spoke sincerely to me of what it meant to be a Christian. Travelling home with my parents at the end of the week my mother asked if I wanted to go on to the EMW conference at Aberystwyth the following week. Knowing that some of my new friends would be there, we agreed to go and see if there was space in the youth camp.

As it happened there was one space left. This was no accident. I anticipated that the week would be a momentous one in my life. Sure enough my conviction of personal sin increased all week, so much so that finally I could do nothing else but look away from myself in order to collapse on Jesus. After all, he it was who had taken the punishment for my every sin on the cross. By his resurrection he both vindicated his saving work and held out to me the promise of a new life. Thus I began to off-load all my cares on to Christ, aware that being alive in Heaven he was ever ready to save me, a sinner on earth.

Possessed of all the knowledge required and stripped of my hypocrisy before God, I spent much of the week in prayer – including the duration of Rev. Luther Rees' sermon on the Thursday evening. At the end of it, Mr. Rees invited any interested in becoming Christians down to the front so that he could speak and pray with them. Mortified by the thought, it was all too easy to refuse the offer. After all, I had caught a glimpse of my mother making her way to the gallery before the service! 'But,' I thought, 'if salvation is God's greatest gift, he may well be testing me to see how much I really want to become a Christian.' It was a struggle, but being a steward at the service that evening it was possible to pretend to check the amplification equipment before slipping through the back into the vestry! There I sat with an older lady and a young man from Swansea, each of whom was lovingly spoken to and prayed for by Mr. Rees.

Needing to be alone with God I quickly left the church to wander prayerfully through the dark streets. God had finally cornered me. All 'ifs' and 'buts' of self-excuse were gone. There was nothing to do but plead with God that he would forgive my sin and accept me as his own forever. It was comparable to the time I had fallen down an inspection chamber as a young boy with only the light above to look for help. 'I cannot demand that God answer me, let alone answer me now,' I reasoned. 'What else can I do for now but try and keep the commandments?' No sooner had the thought been conceived than another came flooding into my mind, 'But that is the point, I can't do it! I need to know that Christ has done it for me.'

In a state of despair I returned to the camp at Penweddyg School and went straight to bed in order to continue wrestling with God. The night was a sleepless one. God's mercy had become everything to me. Nevertheless, with no answer forthcoming, I was ready to give up on God by the morning. My logic was obvious. If God cannot keep his promise that everyone calling upon him will be saved (Acts 2:21) he cannot be God. At that moment I was forcibly struck by one of the many truths learnt in Sunday School. God is omnipresent. That means that he must be with me even in this sleeping bag! I must reach out for him then, because, as the apostle Paul assured the Athenians, he is not far from anyone of us (Acts 17:27).

So with renewed Heaven-sent vigour I got up and went to the morning prayer meeting. There, praise was offered for the three converted the night before. This annoyed me for it appeared presumptuous and was so contrary to my desperation to know, in the words of the hymnist, that 'Jesus is mine'. Life could no longer go on without him. Just as the prayer meeting ended my depression suddenly but quietly lifted. I felt at peace with God. He had heard my prayer and, taking away my sin that stood as a barrier between us, brought me to himself. I walked out into the bright morning sunshine with the cheerful thought ringing in my head, 'so this is real Christianity'. And so it was... and continues to be.

## Life as God's child

That was August 1981. Since then God has perplexed me many a time, but has never let me down or let me go. He employs my daily experiences for my growth in what John Calvin famously described as true and sound wisdom: the knowledge of God and of myself. As he does so, he teaches me about his power and willingness to forgive, heal, and preserve, so that by the time we meet hereafter I shall be like him in holiness and be able to see him as he is (Psalm 17: 15). In the meantime, he calls me to join all his people in loving and serving him in the world. The desire to put God first came slowly. To begin with I revelled in the forgiveness procured by Christ on the cross, but was reticent to forsake the sin for which he was crucified. Consequently, being restless, miserable and unable to see why, I began to cast mental aspersions on the reality of Christianity; that is, until I saw the power of God working very close at hand.

In the crucible of life a Christian's relationship

with God feeds off everyday occurrences, especially those life-shaping turning points such as Dad's diagnosis with Multiple Sclerosis in September 1983. As he woke me for school in the months thereafter I could not help but observe that the diagnosis had made no impact on his cheerful demeanour either within or without the home. For months I wrestled with this until one day, as he left the bedroom, the solution suddenly clicked into place in my mind: 'That's it! There is no true happiness without true holiness! I must seek to walk with God daily if I am to know more of the gospel's joy and peace.' Ever since I have been conscious that the Christian's joy ought to be a holy accompaniment through all circumstances and not just a goal beyond it.

### A 'social oddball' for Christ

Thus I left home for University, set on following God wherever he would lead. As earlier suspected, I was en route to become a 'social oddball' like my father! What eventually turned me towards the ministry was the sheer contrast between my study of politics and the beauty and power of biblical truth expounded at Ebenezer Baptist Church, Swansea. Whereas the one is obviously important for the here and now, the other is vital for now and for eternity. Although both trained my mind, the University lectures left me depressed at the state of the world, but the weekly sermons and fellowship convinced me that God has not left humankind destitute. He has given us 'the Truth', his Son Jesus (John 14:6). By the time the degree was complete my heart felt increasingly compelled to make him known.

Thus, the past nine years of theological training at the Free Church of Scotland College, Edinburgh, and New College, the Divinity Faculty of Edinburgh University, have been spent studying and preaching Christian theology. Rarely do I ascend a pulpit without being driven by an anticipation and expectation that God's Word will achieve its divinely intended purpose (Isaiah 55: 11). If my own sin can prove to be the greatest hindrance to my preaching, the consciousness of it is a powerful stimulus in commending the Saviour to fellow sinners. When God uses a sermon to take a person from where he is to where in Christ he ought to be, then my joy is compounded. Conversely, little does more to bring sadness to the work of preaching Christ than witnessing a sinner's indifference to the Saviour so desperately needed.

Recently I moved to Philadelphia to help train others for Christian ministry. Accompanying me across the Atlantic were some favourite words from John Newton: 'I am not what I should be, I am not what I could be, I am not what I shall be hereafter, but I am not what I once was; and, what I am, I am by the grace of God.' It is that grace that took away my 'Churchianity' and gave me Christ; it is that grace that will one day substitute my semi-literate understanding of how God did it, for the full reality of what it means to know him and to be with him and his people forever, without either sin or separation.

# PRITTI GURNEY

I grew up in a Hindu home in Leicester. Although my parents hardly ever visited the temple we did have a small shrine in our lounge. It was at that shrine that I regularly saw my mum burn incense and pray to the statues of the gods.

Hinduism is one of the oldest of all the world religions. It began in India so long ago that there is no record of its beginnings nor of any one person who was its 'founder'. Its roots run deep in Indian people, wherever they are. The Hindu holy book is the Upanishads, which teaches that Brahman (God) is everywhere and in everything that lives. There is a second holy book, the Ramayana, which describes the god Rama's adventures on earth. In a mandir (a Hindu temple) there are statues to many gods. Among them are Lakshmi, the goddess of wealth, and Vishnu, the god who protects from danger.

**Festivals and fun times**

Our home was a happy one. As a child, I enjoyed celebrating the Hindu festivals. There are four main ones. In January, at Saraswati Puja, the goddess Saraswati is honoured. Hindus believe that it is she who gives understanding. Three months later the spring festival, Holi, is held in honour of Krishna. And in September it is Durga Puja. Then the goddess Durga, who looks after the weak, is worshipped. But Divali, the Hindu New Year, which is celebrated at the end of October or beginning of November, is the one I remember best. These festivals were always joyful times of dressing up in new clothes, having big family meals with relatives, and being spoilt by uncles and aunts wanting to give us gifts of money. Occasionally during these times of festival, my younger relatives and myself would also have to burn incense or say a prayer to one of the many Hindu gods, but it didn't mean much to us at all.

When I was about five years old my parents allowed my two older sisters, my younger brother and myself to attend the local Baptist church. I don't know what made them come to that decision. But I do remember that a lot of the children who lived in our multicultural neighbourhood attended. I loved going to church. Before long I was attending Girls' Brigade and any other special events that were held. The congregation was aware of its responsibility to reach out beyond its own membership and it welcomed us all in, whatever our ethnic or religious background. They even had special activities for children during the school holidays.

## Who am I?

As I grew older a battle began to rage in my heart. Was I a Hindu or a Christian? I never doubted that there was a God and that he had created me. And when I looked at the chipped statues of the Hindu gods in our shrine at home I felt they could be nothing more than what they were, chipped statues. But I felt very confused. Was Christianity only for white people? If I were to say I was a Christian would I be denying the fact I was an Indian?

I loved my parents and wanted to please them. Dad and Mum worked hard and sacrificed a lot to bring us up well. They welcomed our church friends into our home and even came to prize-giving services, which must have seemed very alien to them, just to see us receive our awards. My mum was always keen to tell our relatives what we did at church and about how kind the church people were to us, inviting us to their homes and giving us lifts. Although my relatives were happy to support us, they enforced a more traditional Hindu lifestyle on their own children. I think my Indian school friends thought it was a bit strange and I found it awkward telling them I went to church, but none of them ever opposed me.

But life was complicated because I knew in my heart of hearts that I was not the same as the church people anyway. Like them I believed the

Bible message and accepted that Jesus Christ had lived on earth as a man and that he had died on the cross and been raised again. But I knew that they believed it in a different way. Deep inside me there was an emptiness and I felt very confused.

Then my sisters, who were both in their teens, were converted while away with the church at a young people's weekend in 1980. I overheard them telling my parents that they had 'become Christians'. My parents responded surprisingly, 'Well, you do your thing and we'll do ours.' My confusion deepened. There was obviously more to being a Christian than just going to church. But what was it?

Some time afterwards, as I lay on my bed one night, one of my sisters asked me if I knew how to become a Christian. When I told her that I did not she explained the real message of the gospel to me. I already knew Jesus had been crucified, I heard that every week in church, but I began to realise for the first time in my life that he had died for me. The truth of it all began to sink in, that when Jesus hung and died on the cross he was there in my place, bearing the guilt of my sin. My young mind and heart took in something of the wonder of it and I knew I needed to thank him for what he had done and to say sorry to him for my sin that had caused him so much pain. It was as if I had been blind and God was opening my eyes to see the way to himself.

**Jesus died for me, Pritti.**
Just a few weeks later I met him for myself. It was a Sunday evening and I sat in the front row of the church for the evening service. I can still remember how I felt my heart burn inside me as I heard again of God's love in sending Jesus to die in my place on the cross. I knew then I had to repent and turn to Christ, and I had to do it there and then. That night, 13th May 1984, at the age of fourteen and after talking to an older Christian, I prayed and trusted Christ as my Saviour.

Looking back, that was the greatest moment of my life. When my mum came to pick me up after church I blurted out that I too had become a Christian. She didn't say much, but probably thought, 'Oh, no, not another one!' That night as I went to sleep, it was as though life suddenly made sense. I belonged to God who had forgiven me and promised me eternal life. He had created me to be what I was, Indian and a child of God. The Bible says, 'But now, this is what the Lord says – he who created you, O Jacob, he who formed you, O Israel: "Fear not, for I have redeemed you; I have called you by name; you are mine"' (Isaiah 43:1). And that was my experience!

Then followed my first day at school as a Christian. God gave me real boldness, enabling me to tell my friends about the new life I had found in Christ. Most of them were keen to listen.

Some even came along to witness my baptism three months later. I began to experience God's power in my life in ways I, and others, could see. Before my conversion I swore a lot, but even in these early days of faith God was changing me, helping me to speak words that were pleasing to him.

## The learning process

As a young Christian, I was introduced to Leicester Young Life, an interdenominational youth group, that met in the home of a Christian couple. There I was introduced to other young people who wanted to live for the Lord. Through lively programmes and Bible studies each Friday and Saturday evening, I learned about the importance of spending time alone with my heavenly Father each day. If I was to grow as a believer, I needed to talk to God in prayer and to listen to him speaking to me as I read his word, the Bible. There was nothing superficial in this learning process, rather I was getting to know the Lord as a person.

Young Life also made me aware of the great spiritual need of those who had not heard and accepted the Good News about the Saviour Jesus. As a result I spent some of my summer holidays on United Beach Missions, trying to share the gospel with holidaymakers. Throughout the year, Young Life used open-air meetings in Leicester's city centre as outreach. Sometimes this was hard, and people laughed at us or made it clear that, where Jesus was concerned, they just didn't want to know. They had no idea how desperate their need for him was.

Aged sixteen, I left school and went to a sixth form college to do my 'A' levels. As I had always wanted to be a primary school teacher, when in the upper-sixth, I applied to universities in London to do my teacher training. All set though I was to go to London, I didn't get the results I needed and had to go through my 'A' levels and the application procedure again the following year. That was a difficult time for me, as I watched friends leaving Leicester for university. I felt such a failure. But the Lord knew I had much to learn, and nothing that happened was outside of his control. God's Word speaks to his people at such times. '"For I know the plans I have for you," declares the Lord, "plans to prosper you and not to harm you, plans to give you hope and a future"' (Jeremiah 29:11).

## Student life

During that year the Lord changed my desire to go to London and I found myself applying to universities in the north of England. Eventually, in September 1989, I began a teaching training degree, specialising in Art, Design and Technology at Leeds Metropolitan University.

The four years that followed were among the happiest of my life. There was so much to learn at university. And God very patiently taught me much in the University of Christian living.

One of the lessons I had to learn regarded compromise. In my first year I lived in halls of residence where it would have been so easy to slip into the lifestyle of many of my fellow students, who seemed to live to consume quantities of alcohol and to engage in immoral relationships. But God was my companion, and he helped me to live my life for him. Then, for three years, I shared a house with six other girls. These wonderful friends became like sisters to me. We had many laughs together, and some of the pranks we got up to could only be described as utterly crazy!

The University Christian Union was a real blessing to me. It was there I learned the joy of working with Christians from very different backgrounds and with a variety of viewpoints. What we had in common was the knowledge that Jesus had died for us and now lived within us, urging us to tell our student friends about the new life we had found in him.

Much though I loved student life, it eventually came to an end at my graduation in 1993. But a testing time was to follow. A keen, newly qualified primary school teacher I certainly was, but there was no queue of schools waiting to employ me and I was fortunate to find supply work and did that for a term. During that time I felt God was asking me if I was willing to trust him, even if his way of doing things was different from my dreams.

In his perfect time, the Lord did provide just the right job for me and I worked for three and a half years as a teacher in Leeds, in a good primary school with a highly committed staff. What a lot of satisfaction there was in having a new class of children each September and seeing them develop and mature over the year. I found I could always rely on God for the patience I needed to deal with the children fairly, and the wisdom to treat them as individuals with different talents and needs.

## Meet Marcus

It was after graduating that I met Marcus. He had been brought up in a Christian home in the Yorkshire Dales and had become a Christian at the age of eleven. After leaving school, he joined the family's building business and worked in it for ten years before beginning a course at Durham University in Chinese Studies.

According to Marcus, he first saw me at a Christian Conference about missionary work some four years earlier. From then, until we met in the summer of 1993, he prayed that God would bring us together. I saw him at a lot of Christian events but never had the opportunity to speak to him. Despite that, I felt attracted to him and began to pray that God, if it was his will, would allow us to get to know each other.

As part of his university course, Marcus went away to spend a year in China, a country that had held a fascination for him for several years. Whilst in China, unbeknown to me, he received a letter from a mutual friend (who was sworn to secrecy by both of us!) hinting about my interest in him. On learning that, Marcus wrote to me and so our correspondence began. It was a surprise to his family and friends when he returned home unexpectedly for a Christmas visit. But it was not a surprise to me, for I was there to meet him officially for the first time at Heathrow Airport!

Over that holiday we spent a lot of time getting to know each other as friends. God graciously and clearly confirmed his will to us, that we should become life partners, man and wife. But there were things to do first. Marcus returned to China to complete his university year and I taught. Easter was a treat: I spent it in China with him. And a year later, at Easter 1995, we were married. We believe that our Heavenly Father brought us together in an unusual and amazing way, and we thank him for his goodness to us then and ever since.

On his return from China, God led Marcus back into the family building firm, and he has remained there. We now live near Wetherby and worship God at the King's Church in Boston Spa. The congregation there really is a family and we derive great encouragement from our fellow members. It is our privilege to serve the Lord by teaching in Sunday School together and by running a youth club during the week. Both Marcus and I have a deep desire to see children and teenagers turn to Christ early in their lives, thus having the experience of his friendship as they grow up and face life's joys and trials.

## An open home

At present I am thoroughly enjoying being a housewife and having time to invest more in our home life. God is opening up new opportunities for me to serve him, both by befriending and offering a helping hand to those who don't yet know him, and by having fellowship and giving encouragement to, and being encouraged by, those who do. And I'm enjoying myself too, creating the design and decor of some of the show houses built by the business.

Marcus and I are so grateful to God for saving us and giving us new life through the death and resurrection of our Lord Jesus Christ. He has been totally faithful to us, even when we have failed him. And he has enabled us to prove that he is the reality in every circumstance of life. Our prayer is that we will be obedient to him, doing whatever he calls us to do and going wherever he calls us to go. And we look forward to that day when we will see him face to face. 'For God so loved the world that he gave his one and only Son, that whoever believes in him shall not perish but have eternal life' (John 3:16). That is our past experience, our present assurance and our eternal hope.

Hindu people also accept there is life after death, because they believe in reincarnation. If they keep the ten rules for living: Don't destroy or injure anything, lie, steal, be envious, be greedy and do keep yourself clean, be contented, be kind and patient, educate yourself and try to give your mind to Brahman, they believe they will go straight to God. But if they have not lived by the ten rules their hope is to be reborn in another form of life. And if they have lived bad lives they might even come back as an animal.

How different is my hope as a Christian! What do I look forward to? The Bible tells me through John's vision of heaven. 'Then I saw a new heaven and a new earth, for the first heaven and the first earth had passed away, and there was no longer any sea. I saw the Holy City, the new Jerusalem, coming down out of heaven from God, prepared as a bride beautifully dressed for her husband. And I heard a loud voice from the throne saying, "Now the dwelling of God is with men, and he will live with them. They will be his people, and God himself will be with them and be their God. He will wipe every tear from their eyes. There will be no more death or mourning or crying or pain, for the old order of things has passed away"' (Revelation 21:1-4).

# BOB AKROYD

I was born in New Jersey in the United States of America in 1966. We were a family of four, Dad, Mom and my younger sister, Nancy. Dad worked most of his life for the Telephone Company and Mom was a teacher at the local school for the deaf. Adopted by my parents when I was just six months old, I have never met my biological parents. But my 'real' parents could not have been more loving, caring, nurturing and supportive. My sister, who is three and a half years younger than me, was also adopted. Our upbringing proves how much good can be done by couples who adopt children. We had a happy and fun-filled childhood. My favourite memories are of the New Jersey shore where my parents have a summer home. We went to Surf City on Long Beach Island to swim, play miniature golf and generally enjoy the hot weather. Dad is a keen fisherman and I remember many dark mornings when we rose early to go out on the ocean in search of flounder and weakfish.

Possibly because my mother is a teacher herself, I have always enjoyed school. Studying and reading were never a chore. Although I was not exactly sure what I wanted to be when I grew up, I knew that I wanted to do something meaningful with my life, something both for myself and for others. After graduating from High School in Lawrence, New Jersey, I studied American History at the University of Virginia. This beautiful university is located in Charlottesville, a lovely town in the foothills of the Blue Ridge Mountains. There I met many lifelong friends. In 1988, when I graduated, I did not know what the next step in my life would be. Then a good friend invited me to go with him to live and work in Japan. So off I went to Tokyo, one of the largest and most crowded cities in the world. Very quickly I found a job with a British company, teaching English to Japanese businessmen. I lived in Tokyo for two years and greatly appreciated the opportunity to experience a culture vastly different from my own and to visit such exotic places as Malaysia, Singapore, Hong Kong, and China.

## On the move again

Although I enjoyed teaching very much, I realised that happy as I was during my time there, Japan was not to be my permanent home. A friend, my eye-doctor, who knew I was considering my future, said, 'If I were young again, I would love to study in Scotland.' That got me thinking. I found out as much as I could about Scottish universities and I decided that Edinburgh was the place for me. So, in September 1990, I arrived in Waverley Station, Edinburgh, very tired and not knowing a single person in the city.

I clearly remember being met off the train by a young man, Rod, who gave me a cup of coffee and provided some information about Edinburgh and the university. I was directed to a taxi and made my way to the Pollock Halls of Residence where I was to spend my first week in Scotland. I later found out that Rod was a Christian and that he and other members of the Christian Union provided this welcome service to incoming students. Rod and his friends knew what I still had to learn, that service offered in the name of the Lord is never wasted. We may never see the fruits of our labours, but God is true to his Word as Paul insists, 'Therefore, my dear brothers, stand firm. Let nothing move you. Always give yourselves fully to the work of the Lord, because you know that your labour in the Lord is not in vain' (1 Corinthians 15:58).

## Introducing Allen

Aged twenty-three, I was living in another new country and adjusting to another new way of life. And, although the language was the same, the accents were certainly different! The first challenge I encountered was not cultural, however, but practical. I had nowhere to stay. My assumption had been that I would check in at the University Accommodation Office and be given keys to my very own flat. The reality was rather different. I was given instead a list of bedsits and shared flats and I began the process of phoning round landlords in an effort to secure a place to live. I had no success, but at least I was not alone. Of the group of us at the halls of residence who ate breakfast together, many others were also having difficulties finding accommodation.

During these first days in Edinburgh, I became friendly with one guy in particular, Allen Levi, a fellow American, but from Georgia in the deep south. We decided that since we were having no luck on our own, we would pool our resources and look together for a flat for two. The first place we visited was a tiny attic flat on Cockburn Street, right in the middle of Edinburgh's Old Town. The landlady was marvellously idiosyncratic and, after a brief discussion, we agreed to take the flat. What it lacked in space it certainly made up for in character. Allen became one of the most influential people in my life. He was the first person I met who was a 'real' Christian. His religion was his life, not just an activity to engage in on Sunday mornings. To my amazement he always said grace before meals, he read the Bible and, what's more, he seemed to enjoy it! Allen went to church every Sunday, to the morning AND the evening services. I had thought that the sermon was the same at both services to allow those attending to choose which time was most suitable!

## Down to work

It was time to get down to some studying. I came with a very vague idea of comparing Irish and Scottish nationalism, intrigued as I was by Irish history, particularly by the Home Rule movement under the leadership of Charles Stewart Parnell. Since biography was my favourite reading, I was very encouraged when my supervisor, Owen Dudley Edwards, suggested that I focus on the Earl of Rosebery. You haven't heard of him? He was a complete stranger to me too! But my ignorance did not last for long. I soon found out that he was twice Foreign Secretary and, for a little more than a year, he served as Prime Minister. For my purposes he was the single most influential Scottish political figure of his century.

God has been good to me, placing the right people in my life with perfect timing. I had little idea of what postgraduate studies entailed but, having Owen as supervisor and friend, even the difficult times became enjoyable. He has given me a lot of valuable advice over the years. When, for example, I was lecturing for the first time to a first year university class, he said, 'Robert, show how much you love your subject!' That fine advice regarding lecturing is now standing me in good stead in the pulpit. But I'm running ahead of my story! I began to work in earnest, my research taking me to many parts of Scotland, England and Ireland. Five and a half years later I graduated from the University of Edinburgh with a PhD for my thesis entitled, 'Lord Rosebery and Scottish Nationalism, 1868-1896.'

One reason my three year course ended up taking five and a half years was that as well as studying I had a part time job and I also travelled as much as I could in Scotland and throughout Europe. This was an exciting time in my life and in many ways everything was going wonderfully well. I was studying what I was interested in and I even received a scholarship. For the first time ever I was being paid to study! I had a fine group of friends both in Scotland and in the United States. My family was in good health and there seemed to be nothing missing. However, I began to realise that Jesus' words to the rich young ruler were applicable to me as well, 'One thing you lack' (Mark 10:21). My life seemed complete in many ways but, because God was not in it, it wasn't complete at all.

### Jesus, who is he?
It was during my time in Edinburgh that I first began to consider questions like 'Who is this person Jesus?' and 'What is so special about him?' I remember Allen told me how much he

enjoyed church and how interesting the minister was. That hit me. Words like 'enjoy' and 'interesting' were not generally associated with church in my mind. Then one weekend Allen invited me to go to a service with him. I had no reason to say 'no'. In fact, I was quite interested. So I agreed to accompany him. We went to Buccleuch and Greyfriars Free Church of Scotland, near Edinburgh University. This was the first time apart from weddings that I had been in a church for nearly twelve years. I had gone to Sunday school as a child but, after I was confirmed at the age of twelve, I saw no further reason to continue attending. I just stopped going. So, for the first time as an adult, I went to church on Sunday morning.

My initial impression of the service was: this is unusual. In the Free Church of Scotland they generally stand to pray and sit to sing. It seemed as though everything was backwards. But what first struck me was the length of the opening prayer – it seemed like an eternity. I realised that it wasn't all that long because the sermon lasted even longer! I can still remember that morning's text. It was from Psalm 14:1, 'The fool says in his heart, "There is no God."' I knew that the preacher (his name is Donald Macleod and he has since taught me Systematic Theology at the Free Church College) was speaking directly to me because I didn't really believe that there was a God. And what if he did exist? I reckoned it didn't much matter either way. Yet I was interested by what the man had to say, perhaps in part because I was aware that here was an intelligent and educated man who not only believed what he was saying, but he wanted me to believe it as well.

## Going to church, and enjoying it!

I began to attend church on an infrequent basis. This continued, and over the next year my attendance became more regular until I found myself going to Buccleuch and Greyfriars Free Church on Sunday mornings and Holyrood Abbey Church of Scotland in the evenings. And, guess what? I actually enjoyed going to church! As I met Christian people I realised that they were in all walks of life. Prior to that revelation, I thought that if you were intelligent or talented you didn't need to be interested in religion! The two were, to my mind, almost mutually exclusive. In addition to going to church I began to read the Bible for the first time in my life.

After eighteen months in Scotland, Allen left to return home to America. Among the books which he left behind was a copy of the New International Student Bible. One day I came across this, picked it up and I just couldn't believe it, I was reading the Bible and understanding what it was about! This version also contained background information to explain the order of events and the reasons why each book was written – which was very helpful for someone who knew little biblical history. However, though I was reading the Bible and even praying at times, I knew in my heart that I still wasn't a Christian. There were so many unanswered questions. 'Does God exist?' If so, 'Why is there so much evil and suffering in the world?' And, as a historian, I wondered whether the Bible was a reliable record or just folklore. Two vacations served to put these questions into sharper focus.

## Overwhelmed

In 1992, a good friend, Tim, was living in Poland for the summer and Allen's brother, Gary was working as a missionary in Spain. First, I went to Poland in July. Tim and I wanted to see Auschwitz, the notorious concentration camp. We spent a few days in the beautiful city of Krakow and then took a bus to the camp. I was overwhelmed by the sheer size and scale of the place as well as the scope of evil of it all. Display cases filled with children's shoes and spectacles were a poignant reminder of the horrors that had happened there. Ironically, there was a beauty about the place because wild flowers were growing in between the barracks, giving colour to an otherwise desperately depressing place. For me it seemed that here at Auschwitz was concrete proof that there could be no God, certainly not a loving or benevolent God. If such a God existed how could so many men, women and children die so cruelly? That night, I remember having a long and heated discussion with Tim who maintained that there must be a God. He wasn't sure why, but the idea of atheism seemed impossible to him.

## Question time

The following month found me visiting Gary in Spain. He had been a missionary there for several years. During our week together, while sightseeing, we had many interesting conversations. Gary was more 'aggressive' than his older brother. Allen spoke about Christianity when it came up in conversation, but Gary tended to bring up the subject more directly. I didn't mind either approach and by this point I was willing to ask and answer questions about Christianity. One evening, a friend of Gary's, Felix from Madrid, came over and we had a lovely meal together. Gary acted as translator and Felix and I talked about many things. He asked questions about Scotland and my studies and then, out of nowhere, he asked, 'Do you believe in the resurrection of Jesus Christ?' To this I honestly responded, 'I don't know. As I was not a witness I can neither say. "Yes, it happened." nor can I say "No, it didn't happen."'

The conversation which followed made it clear to me that this was the heart of the Christian message. If Jesus did not rise, then faith was pointless. But, if he did rise from the dead, how else could that be explained apart from accepting that he really was who he said he was, the Son of God. This brought me back to the question, 'Was the Bible reliable?' Felix concluded our conversation by saying that he could not convince me that Jesus had risen, but shouldn't I consider the record which was left, that is the Bible, and draw my own conclusions? My mind-set changed. Rather than relying on what other people said about the Bible, I began to consider what the Bible said itself.

**Light begins to dawn**
In September, I visited Allen back at his home in Georgia, where again I had the opportunity to ask questions and meet other Christians. When I first gave serious consideration to Christianity, I had asked myself, 'Why should I believe in Jesus?' But, by the autumn of 1992, I found myself beginning to ask questions like, 'Why am I not believing in Jesus?' 'Do I have a good case for not being a Christian?' While in Georgia, I heard a cassette tape of Charles Colson speaking to students at Harvard University. I only knew about Colson with regard to the Watergate scandal. What I didn't know was that, while he

was in prison following Watergate, he had become a Christian. He was speaking on the tape about the problem of pain and suffering in the world and, in the course of his talk, he addressed the problem of the holocaust. For the first time I realised that God was not responsible for the death of those six million Jews, but rather men and women, 'ordinary' people, were responsible either by their actions or by their inaction. I began to understand that the problems of this world are not caused by God but by man.

**That's it!**
My interest was raised. I continued going to church twice a week and reading the Bible, even taking notes! But I was still not a Christian. Then one cold January evening in 1993, I was listening to a tape of Douglas MacMillan, the late minister of Buccleuch and Greyfriars. He was preaching about the wise men who came from the east when Jesus was born. His text was, 'Where is the one who has been born king of the Jews? We saw his star in the east and have come to worship him' (Matthew 2:2). As I listened I realised that the wise men were the exact opposite of me. They knew very little about Jesus, but what little they did know they acted upon. Whereas, I knew quite a lot about Jesus, but was more like the scribes and teachers of the law in the story. They were able to say from their knowledge of the Old

Testament where Jesus would be born, but had no interest whatever in going to Bethlehem to see him for themselves. The wise men wanted to worship the King. I knew then what it meant to be a Christian: it meant worshipping the King of Kings. That night, I acted upon what I knew and trusted in Jesus. I didn't know all that it meant or implied but I did know that David's words were true for me that day and for all the days to come, 'Surely goodness and love will follow me all the days of my life, and I will dwell in the house of the LORD for ever' (Psalm 23:6).

Six months after my conversion, I was asked to help out at a summer mission in Lossiemouth, on the Moray coast, and that was a real help to me as a young Christian. I learned so much from my fellow team members, and from the Christians we worked with in Lossiemouth, about what it meant to be a Christian in day to day life. Back in Edinburgh, I became involved in a Sunday morning service for homeless people run by Carrubers Christian Mission. This was a chance to serve the physical and spiritual needs of men and women who were homeless, hungry and hopeless. Through that, I came in contact with Bethany Christian Trust.

**Volunteers please**
A few months later, in 1994, there was an appeal in church for volunteers to help at Bethany House,

a new shelter for homeless people in Leith. With much fear and trepidation, I went down on a Monday night to visit the residents there and I must admit that I have never felt less comfortable. I thought that visit to Bethany House was my first and last. But as we prepared to leave, John, one of the project workers, said, 'Thank you so much for coming. We really appreciate all that you've done. When are you coming again?' I heard myself say, 'Next week,' and I have been going there ever since! John truly gave a word in season, and it was just the encouragement I needed. I look back with gratitude at the way in which God has used my experiences at Bethany to strengthen my faith and to show me what Christian service really means. Many friends from Bethany have come to church and, as a result of this visitation, many people now know the gospel message even though as yet they are not Christians.

Over the past three years (1996-1999), I have been working for my congregation, Buccleuch and Greyfriars Free Church, as an outreach worker. This involves visiting people in the community, at Bethany House and in local prisons. These are great opportunities which bring even greater challenges. How can we present the Christian message in a meaningful way to people who have no background knowledge at all? How can we meet physical needs while also addressing the spiritual problems which lie at the root of social ill? These are questions which have stretched me and caused me to grow and, I hope, mature as a Christian. With this practical experience, I began to consider full time Christian service.

## God is gracious!

In 1996, I entered the Free Church College from which I graduated in May 1999, the same month in which I married Heather Johnston, who is also a member of Buccleuch and Greyfriars Free Church. Heather and I first met when we both volunteered to visit Bethany House. God is gracious! And, on 21st August, 1999, I was ordained as a minister and appointed assistant to Rev. Alex MacDonald in my home congregation of Buccleuch. I came to Scotland to study history, and I remain here to preach his story, the message of God's redemption through the Lord Jesus Christ.

As I look back, I can echo the words of David, 'The boundary lines have fallen for me in pleasant places; surely I have a delightful inheritance' (Psalm 16:6). I have learned that God meets us where we are and he takes us to where he wants us to be. He leads and guides by his Word and by the situations he places us in. My life has been marked by joy and happiness; true, there have been tears and trying times, but they have been the exception rather than the rule. I have tasted and have seen that God is good, and I hope and pray that he will continue to allow me to tell others of his goodness and demonstrate in my life the reality of his grace.

# INDEX

Four subjects, Bible study, prayer, conviction
of sin and guidance, come up to some degree or
other in most chapters of the book.  Some of
the other subjects covered can be found in the
accounts indicated below.

| | |
|---|---|
| **Marriage problems** | Barbara Ladds |
| **Ministers' wives** | Morwen Higham, Lindsay Benn |
| **Ministry** | Liam Goligher, Christopher Idle, Joel Edwards, Tim Trumper, Bob Akroyd |
| **Missionary life** | Marie-Christine Lux |
| **Racial issues** | Joel Edwards, Pritti Gurney |
| **Religious or Christian** | Morwen Higham, Tim Trumper |
| **Roman Catholic background** | Oliver McAllister |
| **Serving God as a scientist** | Ghillean Prance |
| **Spiritual darkness** | Marie-Christine Lux |
| **Teenage rebellion** | Barbara Ladds |

Christian Focus Publications publishes biblically-accurate books for adults and children. The books in the adult range are published in three imprints.

*Christian Heritage* contains classic writings from the past.

*Christian Focus* contains popular works including biographies, commentaries, doctrine, and Christian living.

*Mentor* focuses on books written at a level suitable for Bible College and seminary students, pastors, and others; the imprint includes commentaries, doctrinal studies, examination of current issues, and church history.

For a free catalogue of all our titles, please write to
Christian Focus Publications,
Geanies House, Fearn,
Ross-shire, IV20 1TW, Great Britain

For details of our titles visit us on our web site
http://www.christianfocus.com